LOVE

Straight From

THE HEART

Norma Iris Pagan Morales

ISBN 978-1-959895-92-3 (paperback)
ISBN 978-1-959895-91-6 (ebook)

Printed in the United States of America

Dedication

This is dedicated to my sister, ADELIN MILAGROS PAGAN MORALES. She is gone but not forgotten. Thank you, sis for always praising my work.

Overview

Time seemed to freeze for a moment. His eyes are the type you can lose yourself in, in a heartbeat. They were kind and welcoming. You know how you sometimes get a feeling about someone, just by looking into the windows of their soul. With him, I felt nothing but genuine comfort and sincerity.

I snapped out of my sudden trance to respond. He was now no more than an arm's length away from me. As I began to converse with him, within the moment of a snap, everything around me faded away to complete darkness; but then I heard a door open and a voice.

"How are you? Still in bed! You've nonstop been the talk downstairs. You know how important today is. You've got about 30 minutes, before your absence will be fully noticed by more than just me." She proceeded to say, while opening all my curtains.

Contents

Dedication iii

Overview v

Chapter 1.   Just Dreams 1

Chapter 2.   Damn Hunger 5

Chapter 3.   The Lessons from the Future 10

Chapter 4.   Heartache Special 17

Chapter 5.   Fate 24

Chapter 6.   Worse Than Death 29

Chapter 7.   I'm The Only One 40

Chapter 8.   If The Shoe Fits 44

Chapter 9.   Seeing You 48

Chapter 10. What if 53

Chapter 11. Letters I Can't Write 59

Chapter 12. In another Time 64

Chapter 13. Breaking Up is Hard to Do 73

Chapter 14. In Another Love Life 80

Chapter 15. Good Love 85

Chapter 16. Last Wish 93

Chapter 17. Not Meant to Be 102

Chapter 18. Love That Kills Never Dies 107

Chapter 19. The Origin of Short Stories..112

Chapter 20. Early Examples of short stories....................................116

Chapter 21. Characteristics of a Short Story 123

References 127

About the Author..131

Chapter 1

Just Dreams

My dreams always the same....

I always began to walk through a strange forest. I was always lost, looking for something.

For a time, I thought I heard a faint calling in the distance. It almost sounded like a name...my name? I couldn't quite make out the words though, along with the direction the voice came from.

I did not have the energy to make my presence known, shouting back, "I'm here, over here!" The shouts became more spaced, until the last call. Now there's only silence.

I must have wandered for hours now. Night had come, and navigation was nearly impossible now.

I had no compass, no map, and no view of the heavenly lights. The towering trees had such a thick overhead, it blocked most of the light trying to pierce through. I'd see occasionally floating light bugs here and there, but as I neared any they'd rapidly disperse.

I'd catch glimpses of the landscape they illuminated; it was breathtaking and unreal.

I thought early on to retrace my steps, but it was near impossible now. I could not see further than 6ft ahead or behind. I wasn't walking on any clearcut paths.

I began coming to terms with the reality of my situation. I sat down against some random tree and uncontrollably started crying.

I'm not sure how much time passed, as I sat there on the ground. I heard a rustling noise.

It was faint at first but was getting remarkably louder along with a heaving breath. I then I noticed the glowing eyes coming towards me.

I frantically got up and turned to run, but next thing I know, I'm knocked down to the ground. I turn around to see my attackers face, only to be met with a very anxious dog.

The lack of light made it difficult to make out her breed, as well as check her collar for a name. I was certain of her being female though.

"Hey girl, where'd you come from?"

She just looked at me with her doe eyes. She seemed kind enough. I was confused by her sudden appearance, but my relief outweighed the concern. I pet her for a bit while she caught her breath. Suddenly she hopped out of my hold to leave, from the direction she came.

I kept my eyes on her. After a few paces forward, she stopped and looked back. I remained in the same spot. She continued a few more paces but noticed my stillness, stopped again, waiting no more than a few seconds this time before running back to me. She nudged me to get up.

I thought to myself, stay here lost and alone, or take a leap of faith with this new companion? I don't know how to explain the feeling of sincerity and comfort I got from her.

I looked her in the eyes and asked, "Are you wanting me to follow? To come with you?"

She responded with an eagerly wagging tail.

"Ok, let's go."

In saying that, she pulled away from me again to follow her, and this time I did.

After walking for some time, we came to the edge of the woods upon an open clearing. I paused for a moment to take in this new view before me.

With the towering trees now behind, the full moon's glory illuminated the beauty of all the surrounding landscape. It kind of looked like a vineyard or orchard of a sort before me.

The grid was peculiar, structured in a way to hide whatever lay beyond it. There were some flickering lights spread out here and there. They looked too large to be lightning bugs.

As we trekked on to the edge of the grid, my companion came to sudden stop, perking her ears. Within a few minutes, I began to hear it too. My heart raced.

There was not enough time to run back uphill from whence we came. So, I stood there, frozen.

I couldn't read her well. She seemed adamant to stay where we were but gave no clear signs of fear or excitement for what was coming. The moving lights were clearer. They were lanterns.

A small group of men on horses and their hounds approached us. They all stopped a good distance from us, making room for a man to come from their midst.

I didn't possess much on their faces, until I saw him. He looked no different than the others in attire and stature. They all had varying likeness to him specifically, yet all had a distinct feature apart from each other.

His hair though, no man likened to. It appeared to be intentionally distinct. It was dark, long, and like wool. He dismounted from his horse, handing one of the reigns to the nearest man on his right. I heard a deep voice call out.

In hearing that man's voice, my companion looked at me waiting a moment, then eagerly left my side for him.

They appeared familiar with each other. He then fixed his gaze on me, locking his eyes on mine.

"Ray, is that you?" He said in a shaky, stunned tone.

Time seemed to freeze for a moment. His eyes are the type you can lose yourself in, in a heartbeat. They were kind and welcoming. You know how you sometimes get a feeling about someone, just by looking into the windows of their soul. With him, I felt nothing but genuine comfort and sincerity.

I snapped out of my sudden trance to respond. He was now no more than an arm's length away from me. As I began to converse with him, within the moment of a snap, everything around me faded away to complete darkness; but then I heard a door open and a voice.

"How are you? Still in bed! You've nonstop been the talk downstairs. You know how important today is. You've got about 30 minutes, before your absence will be fully noticed by more than just me." She proceeded say, while opening all my curtains and windows. "The fresh air will do you some good," she said as she turned from the last window, heading back to the main door.

"I had the dream again."

She stopped in her tracks.

"It was different this time. I could clearly see his face, and he spoke to me like we were familiar."

She remained calm. Then turned and said, "We can talk about it later. Right now, you need to get ready. Your mother will not live this down if today is anything short of perfect." In making that statement she abruptly left my room closing the door. I waited until her footsteps receded before getting out of bed.

Last night was sudden. I had not had that recurring dream since the incident. Something must be wrong. What are they not telling me? As I started getting ready, I kept replaying our interaction in my head. There had to be some clue or symbol I was missing. Then it hit me. I know that crest.

Chapter 2

Damn Hunger

The music was so loud, you could feel it in your chest the moment you walked in.

The loud bass had everyone moving; even those by the bar just casually having a conversation or trying to get the bartender's attention.

Juanita let out a breath as she looked around; the lights had a neon effect on them as she was pulled by her friend, Nicole, to the bar.

"What are you drinking?!" She looks over at her, letting out a breath. "Uh…A tequila sunrise!" Nicole had yelled to the bartender about hers and Juanita's drinks as Juanita looked around again.

"He's the best around!" "Who?!" "The DJ; Mike J, the best. We are so lucky to see him tonight!" Juanita nodded as she wasn't even aware of that.

Coming out to Echo hadn't been her first choice but it's Friday night and she's only in town for a few days before having to travel back to Montana.

She had her friend of 10+ years drag her to her favorite club in Silver Heights. Nicole handed her drink as she took a sip. The tequila was strong, the orange juice doing very little to help but still… Good drink.

Juanita could feel her hips swaying to the music as she let out a breath, taking another sip of her drink as Nicole smiled at her.

"Shots!" Before Juanita could protest, Nicole was ordering shots as Juanita shook her head, looking back onto the dance floor.

She could see people grinding against each other as bodies fell into natural rhythm; almost like it was just natural for them to fall and move against each other.

"Here! "Juanita lets out a breath as she grabs it; "To us!" "To us!" both click their glasses and take the shots quick and easy.

Juanita gasps as she places her glass on the bar as Nicole does the same. "God… fucking tequila."

Nicole nods as she takes a sip of her water, "yeah." coughs as she shivers as Juanita finishes the rest of her drink just as the beat drops and everyone starts going crazy, Nicole orders two more drinks.

On the other side of the bar, Nick sips his beer. Silver Heights Echo wasn't always his move. Tonight, it felt and seemed different; no douchebag frat guys trying to impress some sorority girl or just douchebags trying to pick a fight to look tough.

No, the crowd was here for one thing and one thing only; to have fun and live a little. Something Nick could get behind as he lets out a breath.

"Hey, going to dance; coming?" Nick looked at Link who he came with, shaking his head. "You go." Link nods as he walks to the dance floor with some girl he was chatting with. As Nick finishes his beer, he looks around the club.

Nick was deciding to get on the floor. He sets his empty bottle on the bar as he walks into the crowd. He started moving as he walked to the bar.

He was letting the music sweep over him starting from his feet to his hips and his chest. God he could feel the bassline in his chest as he started moving.

"Let's go!" Juanita finished her drink and her third shot as she let Nicole take her to the floor.

Juanita let's out a breath as Nicole started jumping and swaying her hips as Juanita started too as well.

Not one for being a dancer; Juanita started just moving her hips as she spanned around and bumped into someone.

"Shit! Sorry!" Gripping their shirt, they grabbed her arms to keep her from falling. "Are you, okay?" She looks at his eyes, as the neon yellow shined. "Whoa." Juanita blinked as she felt her cheeks heat up.

'Thank god for the lights.' She thought as she nodded. "Y-yeah." letting go of his shirt as he let go of her arms. "I'm Nick." Juanita lets out a breath, "Juanita."

Nick had looked at her eyes; the room was blurring as he stared at her. Her full lips had black lipstick that was a bit smudged as he let out a breath.

Her eyes were green and the greenest he'd ever seen. 'How is that possible?' He thought as she bit her bottom lip; causing his lips to drop to her lips. 'Shit.' "Uh. um. You want to dance?"

Juanita had nodded. She thinks she did anyway. Nick had taken her hand and wow. His hand was soft and big. Bigger than hers as he pulled her closer, her chest knocking against his.

"This, okay?" he whispers as Juanita nodded, Nick then spined her around as he gasped. Her back to his chest as he moved her dirty blond hair to the right side he whispered in her ear. "Move."

Nick had felt Juanita start to grind against him. Her ass in his crotch as his hands moved down the sides of her body.

Juanita had moved her head back as he lifted her hands over their hands, as she smiled a bit.

Her body had fallen on fire as she slid down his body. Nick watches her and spins her as she looks up at him biting her lip as she sways her way up to eye level with him as both are panting as they stare at each other.

"Wow…" "Fuck Juanita." Juanita giggles as Nick groans before pulling her closer to him, chest to chest as his hands let go of hers as they travel down her back as her hands wrap around his neck, as he cups her a handful of her ass in his hand causing Juanita to gasp as he smiles.

He lifts her leg as he spins them. Juanita giggles as he lets go over gently as she spins on her feet.

"How the hell didn't I fall?" She thinks as she smiles at him. Nick panting as he stared at her.

This woman who he'd only just met as her hips roll in her black dress that stops mid-thigh as she spined around.

Nick bites her lip as he watched her ass jiggle and roll as she rolled her hips. Nick could see a few catching glimpses as he walked over to her.

Eyeing them in a way that had them quickly looking away as he reaches up to her back as he grabs her hair in his fist causing Juanita to moan.

With the music the sound it is, no one heard it. 'Thank God' she thought as he pulled her to his chest as she smiled.

As they both started moving in sync with each other, his hand stayed in her hair as his left hand had stayed on her hip as hers wrapped around his middle.

As the music changed to energetic dance-pop, Juanita and Nick stayed close. Juanita had realized Nick was wearing a black jumper tucked into his pants.

Juanita had also noticed his high bones, with his nice and full lips. She wants to know how she had become so close to a stranger.

Juanita had no idea how anything happened. It seemed so crazy as she had never had a night like this in her small town. Silver Heights had become something else.

As Nicky had stared at Juanita. Her hair he guessed was half up, but it had become loose, and some strands were framing the sides of her face as her red eyeshadow could only be seen in the blue neon lights as he also noticed the gold on her cheekbones.

"Hey!" he pulls her closer; chest to chest as she wraps her arms around his neck, he tucks a strand of hair behind her ear as he cups her cheek.

"What?!" both are panting as she shakes his head slowly; "who the fuck are you?!" Junita laughs as she shrugs, "I'm just visiting!"

He nods, swallowing the lump in his throat as they stare at each other. Before Nicky leans in and his lips touch Juanita's who moans as she deepens the kiss.

Both groaning as Nicky slips his tongue inside Juanita's mouth.

Chapter 3

The Lessons from the Future

"**B**ad night?"

That would've been obvious to anyone with eyes if the bartender hadn't been so eager about clearing my empties.

I found my reflection in the mirror behind the bar. The glass was so foggy and warped that it turned the scene into an impressionist painting or maybe that was the seven beers I'd just drank. "I am having a bad night."

"I know." The woman I'd never seen before sat down next to me. "You told me to meet you here."

"I don't know you."

"In the future, you do." A fire truck screamed outside, and she paused while it passed. The red lights pulsed in the white bar top, my beer glass, the ice cubes in her drink. "You sent me back here to find you." That was a good hook.

On any other day, that would've sent me scrambling for the Notes app on my phone. I would've put it in a story.

I snuck a glance at her in the mirror. She was pretty, around my age, and had a haircut I couldn't explain. I'd spent my whole life orbiting around people who gave me things to write about.

I'm also very partial to women who hit on me, but I'd just given up writing for good.

10

"Wouldn't telling me about the future create some kind of dimensional paradox?" I asked, dumping the rest of my beer into my mouth. Most of it ended up on my shirt.

"I've been sitting through your lectures on temporal ethics since I was a freshman," she handed me a napkin. "We've worked it all out. Trust me."

I was too drunk for this game. "You've got the wrong guy," I said, crumpling up the napkin without using it. "I'm not a science person."

"Not yet," she insisted. "I'm here to teach you."

I waved at the bartender and paid my bill, but I couldn't ignore the plot holes. "You're here to teach me? You just said I was your professor."

"You were. Now, I'm going to be yours. So, you can be mine."

That would be a mess of a story. "I'm leaving now," I said and stumbled towards the door, holding on to the bar for support like the floor was made of ice and my skates were too big.

I woke up with pizza on my bed. There are worse sleeping companions. I stared at the ceiling, listening to the traffic on 1st Avenue.

The headache pounding against my skull like it was trying to get out. My downstairs neighbors were as always, yelling at each other. My upstairs neighbors as always, having sex.

I knew the rejection letter was still on the floor next to the front door, where I'd left it yesterday.

I'd torn it open, read the first three words, and slammed the door shut behind me. I was already on my way to the bar by the time it hit the floor.

I tiptoed into the kitchen and eyed the letter nervously from a few feet away. I was like afraid it might suddenly charge at me.

If I was rejected from medical school, I'd tell myself that my test scores just weren't high enough. That was a numbers thing.

That it wasn't personal. Being rejected from an MFA program in fiction writing is different. There aren't any numbers to blame it on.

My gaze landed on the picture of Norma that was still on the fridge. If there's an acceptable amount of time to keep a picture of your ex after the breakup, it's long since passed.

Norma hated how I treated my life like it was just material for my stories. The people in it like they were just characters. She said it made her feel used.

"It's never just you and me," she said. "It's you and me and the editorial board of whatever journal you're going to submit the story about us to."

I've never had much of an imagination, never understood how other writers could just invent people in their minds.

I was always looking for things I could steal from reality. Somehow, Norma could tell when I was doing it. She could see it on my face.

"You get this look in your eyes and then it's like you're not even here. Like you shift to some other dimension."

After some trial and error, I discovered that spontaneous acts of free will were the most effective way of convincing Norma that I was there in the moment and not just writing about it in my head.

The more random, the better. I paused in the middle of the intersection on 3rd Avenue and 14th Street while we were walking to Trader Joe's and did a series of circles.

I came up behind her while she was folding laundry and licked her elbow. I shouted, "GIRAFFE!" in the middle of a subway car and then cleared my throat politely like nothing had happened. She liked that stuff. It made her laugh.

I made sure everything I wrote while we were together had nothing to do with her. She read the novella I'd been working on, which was terrible, over breakfast at the kitchen table.

With her feet in my lap, she leaned back and said, "Wow, I had no idea you were into war fiction."

I wasn't. I'm pretty sure most of it was copied from a movie we watched in 11th grade history class. I didn't want to write about the power of friendship in the trenches of World War I.

I wanted to write about the way her hair curled at the back of her neck. I wanted to write about the little noise she made before she said, "Good morning."

I told her that I wouldn't write about her, but all along, somewhere in the back of my mind, I knew that one day I would.

I slammed the lid on the trashcan and retraced my blurry steps from the night before to locate my keys and shoes.

As I bent down to tie my laces, I noticed a large book on the coffee table that hadn't been there yesterday. Unpredictable Predictability: The Cosmology of Theoretical Physics.

I stared at it for a long minute. A breeze whispered through the living room and blew goosebumps down my spine even though all the windows were closed.

A truck honked outside. I jumped a little. I rubbed my face with my hands. I needed coffee, and a bagel.

I was lying on my back in Tompkins Square Park with cream cheese on my face, eyes half-closed against the bright afternoon sky, when suddenly everything went dark.

My first thought was that maybe a meteor was crashing into earth and maybe that wasn't such a bad thing.

I opened my eyes to find the woman from the bar standing over me, blocking out the sun.

"You again?"

"I'm surprised you recognize me," she said. "You were very drunk last night."

"Your haircut is… unique."

"It's trendy in the future."

"I'm sure."

"We need to start studying," she looked like she was trying to remember something she had rehearsed. "You have… potential that you don't see right now."

I sat up slightly. "Did you come home with me last night?"

She made a face. "We're both 23 now," she said. "But in my eyes, you're still my 70-year-old physics professor."

"I'm not playing," I said, refusing to let her know that she had guessed my age exactly right. "There was a textbook on my coffee table this morning. Did you break into my apartment?"

"We don't have time for this," she said. "I have so much to teach you, Hector."

I didn't remember telling her my name.

"How do you…?"

My phone started buzzing. I hung up on the telemarketer and shoved it back into my pocket before turning back to face her.

But she was gone.

I looked around. There were two old men playing chess on a bench nearby. A mom with three children and a dog.

I stood up so I could see further down Avenue A. I caught a glimpse of her weird hair crossing the intersection of E 10th Street.

I started running.

At the end, Norma broke up with me over snow. It was Christmas and we were at her parents' house upstate.

They served dessert and then promptly announced that they were declaring bankruptcy and getting divorced. We barely had a bite of pie.

I never liked seeing Norma cry, but in her childhood bedroom, surrounded by pictures of little Norma, it was even worse.

There were photos of Norma with bangs, Norma with braces and Norma with a cast on her arm.

I held her on the twin-sized bed and thought about all the times she must have cried on that bed when I hadn't been there to hold her.

"There, there," I whispered. For someone who considered themselves a writer, I wasn't great with words. The more emotional a situation, the more I wanted to retreat into my head.

I pulled the blanket up around her shoulders. I tried to blanket her in love. Snow began falling outside, blanketing the lawn… We watched it in silence for a few seconds before she turned to look at my face.

Then she sat up.

"I. Can't. Believe." she said, suddenly shaking with anger instead of with tears.

"What...?"

"Now?" she asked. "Of all times?"

"Now what?"

"You're thinking about a play on words," she said. "Wrapping me in the blanket while the snow blankets the ground outside."

"I'm not," I said. I tried to think of something spontaneous and random I could do to convince her, something I could do to make her laugh, but my mind was blank. "I'm just thinking about you."

"You're not thinking about me," she said, separating herself from the blanket and my arms for the last time. "You're thinking about what you're going to write about me later."

I thought there was some core difference between our ideas about what life and writing were for, but it felt too big to explain right then.

I'd have to write about it first. So, I let her storm off to the guest room and I stayed, wrapped in that blanket, staring at that blanket of snow.

The story I wrote about her wasn't good enough to get her back. It wasn't good enough to get me into grad school, either.

I chased the women to the mouth of the 1st Avenue L station. She was fast and I was hungover, and every passerby seemed doomed to be exactly in my way.

I flew down the stairs, panting, the metallic breath of the subway filling my lungs.

The train doors were already closing by the time I made it onto the platform. I hurled myself between them and most of me made it through.

My foot got stuck. I kicked off my shoe and just left it there, shoving my way through the crowded car, cream cheese still caked around my lips, trying to find her.

The other passengers avoided their eyes, which told me enough about how crazy I looked.

The train pulled out of the station. People pushed against each other. I wound up in a man's lap, muttering apologies behind me as I kept pushing my way through the tangle of bodies, until I finally made it the full length of the car and she wasn't there.

I paused to catch my breath. I rubbed my face with my hands. Maybe I was as crazy as I looked.

I found my reflection on the glass doors. Then, there she was. Right behind me. Waving in the reflection.

I wheeled around.

She wasn't there.

I got off at the next stop and walked home. I was still missing one shoe. I laid down next to the pizza on my bed and stared at the ceiling.

I was trying to decide if I should call a locksmith or a psych ward. If I needed my locks checked, or if I needed to be locked up.

I thought I might have to write about it first.

Chapter 4

Heartache Special

Ever since I can remember, I've dreamed of finding my soulmate. I began looking for him surprisingly young.

It all started with my next-door neighbor, Alex, to whom I wrote a lengthy love letter.

After he shared his chalk with me one hot summer afternoon, I told him we should "get married" but he must not have agreed because he never spoke to me again.

I cried in my mom's arms until she gave me the most important advice I would ever receive: "Sometimes fate makes you wait".

Of course, at 5 years old I didn't understand fate or its infinite wisdom, but I understood what she was trying to tell me. She was telling me that if Alex wasn't my true love, then someone else would be.

My mom and I entrust everything to fate and why shouldn't we? Fate is the only thing that can bring soulmates together, and they come when you least expect it.

My mother certainly wasn't expecting to meet my father when she was scooping ice cream at her summer job when she was 19.

I love hearing the story of how they met, especially because when she tells it her eyes sparkle with excitement, like she's letting me in on a secret.

"I remember it perfectly" she always started theatrically "He came in with a blonde bombshell, but we couldn't stop looking at each other.

He got two scoops of strawberry. She got -" with a shudder for dramatic effect "a small scoop of butter pecan."

The blonde bombshell didn't last long. The next day my dad came back and asked my mom to the movies.

A month later they were married and a year after that I was born. My eyes were just like his according to mom.

Sometimes when she's not home, I pull the small envelope of photographs out from the bottom of her sock drawer.

My favorite picture of him, he is leaning against a shiny red car and smiling widely at the camera. My mom was holding the camera. That is the way I like to imagine it.

As much as I try, I can't quite see his eyes in the picture or in my memory. I racked my mind for any trace of him but as always, it went blank.

It's unsurprising considering he left when I was only 2 years old, but I always try anyway just in case there's a sliver of him hiding somewhere in my subconscious just out of reach.

There are other pictures in the envelope too, of men whose stories I know just as well as I know my father's.

It might be strange, but I take equal comfort in these photos. Julio, my mom's tall and serious prom date whose dark eyes are just as intense in this faded photo as she describes them was holding her hand.

"We simply weren't compatible" she says with a sigh. Not a sad sigh though, my mom tends not to dwell on the past.

When she talks about her lovers of old, she speaks with the breeziness of someone talking about the weather.

She happily tells me of their memories together with me playing the part of fascinated audience member.

Her face beams at the romantic parts, and she shakes her head desperately at the sad parts though it never seems personal, more as if she's telling a fictional story and is expressing the appropriate emotions to enhance the show.

Regardless of how sad their breakup seems she always ends with a reminder: "It just wasn't meant to be. Sometimes fate makes you wait a little bit." Fate has made my mom wait a lot.

After my dad there was Luis, who she dated for two entire years. It seems like an eternity to me, but Mom says two years is just a hiccup in the grand scheme of things.

I can remember Luis. His photo in the little envelope has him tossing me in the air.

When I look at it, I can hear his big booming laugh and my manic high-pitched giggles. It was Luis who comforted me along with my mom after my 2nd grade boyfriend Josie dumped me because he liked another girl.

"He's a fool. Boys never know what they want," He told me firmly "they don't even really think about it until they get older and wiser."

I remember him sharing a small smile with my mom and how badly I wanted to share secrets with someone just by looking at them.

Luis made my mom happy, so I'm not entirely sure why they broke up. My grandma says she cut him loose, but my mom says Luis went to California and she didn't want to go with him.

I can't imagine dating someone for that long and then breaking up. My first major break up was with Oscar.

We had been together for four and a half months when his parents got divorced and he decided to move in with his dad who lived two hours away.

He started going to a different middle school and called me on the phone to tell me he didn't think we should do long distance. I was curled up on the floor clutching the heart shaped necklace he got me when my mom came home from work.

As I choked out the story between sobs, she rubbed my back and told me about how distance can separate adults too. She reminded me about Luis and his dream of moving to California.

She asked me, "What would we have done in California? Our life is here." And she's right.

I wouldn't have wanted to live so far away from Grandma. To cheer me up she treated me to her Heartache Special. Strawberry ice cream topped with chocolate sauce and M&Ms.

The Heartache Special is delicious, but I've never seen my mom have it after one of her breakups.

Since Luis she's had many dates and even a few boyfriends though most only lasted a month or two.

Only one has lasted long enough for me to meet him. I liked Harris. He was a bit older than my mom, with silver hair and a speckled black and gray beard.

He would come over and cook dinner every Friday night. When they first started dating, he would make pasta and fish and sandwiches.

Finally, one night he put his fork down and announced that he couldn't cook for us properly without a grill. I told him we didn't have a grill and the next week a shiny new grill was sitting on our patio.

After that it was all sorts of juicy, tender meat. Mostly steak, which mom and Harris loved.

I liked to sit outside and do my homework while he grilled with my mom next to him.

Every Friday our backyard would smell like savory smoke, and it lingered in our house until the next morning when I would come down for breakfast.

I thought he would move in with us at some point, maybe even be my stepdad. I think Harris thought so too.

Fate had other plans and after one last Friday dinner, they had a hushed argument in the living room. Harris slammed the door on his way out.

I forgot to pretend I wasn't eavesdropping and ran downstairs in tears to check on mom. She had her back to me, and her head bowed low. Her hand was on the doorknob, but she wasn't moving.

Since then, I've speculated that she was deciding whether to go after him. She must've decided not to because she heaved a deep sigh and turned to me with a serene smile and said, "It wasn't meant to be, I guess."

I waited up all night straining my ears for any faint sound of her crying, ready to offer her the Heartache Special.

If she did cry, there was no sign of it because the next day she was her normal cheery self.

She even spent the day rearranging all the furniture in the house. I felt like screaming at her, demanding that she apologize to Harris.

It wouldn't have made any difference, every time I even said his name that week she would interrupt with a reminder to trust in fate.

It was hard for me to trust in fate then. Harris and my mom couldn't have picked a worse time. It was right after I had faced my most painful heartbreak to date.

It was Derek who had eyes as deep as oceans and two dimples on his right cheek. I spent months working up my nerve, analyzing every minute interaction over and over searching for signs of reciprocated feelings.

Every time I spoke to him my thoughts turned into mush. Movies and love songs would automatically call his face to mind.

I had it bad, my mom said. Her advice, as always, was to tell him how I felt. Finally, after rehearsing it in the mirror with myself for a week, I cornered him after class and told him that I really liked him.

Mom advised against using the word love, so I settled for the next best thing.

To my surprise Derek did not reciprocate my feelings. Ever the gentleman, he said he was "flattered" and that I was "a really nice girl".

The worst part wasn't that he didn't like me back, it was how unsurprised he was. Like he had been watching me make a fool of myself for months.

Maybe he had even rehearsed his rejection. It was all too humiliating to bear and then a week later Harris was gone too.

Two heartbreaks in one, and I seemed to be the only one feeling the pain. My mom certainly wasn't fazed, soon after she was putting on her special first date lipstick and curling her hair. The mourning period was over.

I, however, can't recover so quickly. Derek's rejection was a bruise to my pride as well as my heart.

I was starting to lose faith in fate too. I'm only 16, I have plenty of time, but my mom is starting to get silver streaks in her hair.

How could fate ignore someone as open armed as her? Would she have any time left at all by the time she met her soulmate? Had she already met him, and they were just cruelly destined to stay separated?

I spread out the pictures in the envelope again. Jonathan, Trent, my dad, Luis, Phil, Harris. Every photo was alive with emotion, each man gazing adoringly at my mom.

Though she looked different in each one, a few more lines on her face, her cheeks slowly losing the cherub-like effect of youth, her smile was just as radiant. How could she let fate take that feeling away?

I shoved them back into the drawer beneath all the socks and made a promise to myself to never end up like my mom.

If I ever meet someone I love that much, I won't resign myself to fate. My eyes stung with tears but not about Derek this time. Maybe the Heartache Special could cure other types of heartache too.

With an ice cream less freezer I had no choice but to walk down to the grocery store to pick up supplies.

My hair hung limply, and my face was blotchy but for once it didn't matter. The grocery store was nearly empty.

An outdated pop song played halfheartedly over the speaker. Dragging my feet, I dumped everything onto register number 4.

"Tough day?" a male voice snapped me out of my haze. A perfect voice.

The cashier was beautiful. Suddenly my blotchy face felt even blotchier, and my lips yearned for pink lipstick. I gave him my best shy smile.

"You have no idea. What's your name?" I asked.

He grinned and held a handout to shake. "Junior. I just started here last week."

Of course. When I doubted most the universe had other plans. Sometimes fate makes you wait.

Chapter 5

Fate

There is a gruesome fate, a death penalty that is awaiting me, for the crime of being a living, breathing human being with blood rushing through my veins.

I can't stop it. I know that someone is after me. I have been slated for doom since the moment I was born.

I am being hunted through a dark forest by a gruesome monster of myth, simply because, rushing through my veins there is blood.

Blood is the subject of the intrusive thoughts that pour down like rain, hot, sticky, suffocating red rain.

The obsessions that go along with the compulsion to form a disorder are far worse than any creature with too many eyes and limbs and a thirst for blood.

Blood spills on the laundry room floor because dumbass, you didn't make sure the back door was locked.

There must be exactly five stars between the lines I write. If they aren't, the sky will crash down, and the sea will come ashore, and it will all be my fault.

I didn't get any sleep last night, so I woke up before the birds and sat downstairs dark with a stomach full of lead.

My body is so heavy with anxiety and terror that I can't move. I simply sink into the couch, second by second.

This is sleeping immobilization to the max, but unfortunately, I am wide awake. Through yawning and stretching and droopy eyelids, my mind stays alert.

They say there is no rest for the wicked, and this disorder is certainly evil.

Finally, I break through my mental trance and force myself to my feet with stiff limbs and shaking hands.

I take a straight-legged march to the light switch, and with bated breath, watch as the light illuminates my house. Certain someone is crouching there in the dark.

It takes a few minutes for my heart rate to calm down, and then I begin to go about my morning routine.

Milk first, then coffee, and stir seven times. Exactly two pieces of bread go into the toaster, and exactly five eggs are scrambled slowly, methodically, the wooden spatula pushing them back and forth with a dull scraping noise.

When I open the cabinet to get plates, I tap each shelf twice. My husband asks me what I think will happen if I don't. I open my mouth to respond.

'Something bad,' I would say. 'So bad I don't understand what it is.' Then I close my mouth, realizing I don't know.

I don't if my husband will leave me. My luck will run out and everything I've ever loved will disappear and it will be all my fault.

Work is hell, but what else is new? I am lost, swallowed by the clicking of a mouse and drowned in a sea of blue light that has risen so high, it now laps against the membrane of my eyes.

I slam my laptop closed and the water quickly recedes, leaving salt crusted on my eyes, making them feel itchy and dry.

I lean back in my spinning chair, taking a breath for what feels like the first time in hours. After all, when you are drowning, it's hard to breathe.

As I stand, I am engulfed in a different kind of ocean. I am in danger.

My fate was written long ago, and it will soon be fulfilled. My mind works that way. Inside my head, the skies were always, always cloudy, and whenever I paid any attention, whenever anyone said, 'looks like rain,' the hot, sticky drops of red blood began to pour down.

I could change it. Someone would crawl into my office window and slit my neck. I checked the window to see that it was locked.

The first section ended with three words, so every section that follows must do the same or my world will crumble out from underneath me.

I will lose my job and my money and every opportunity I have ever been presented with, and it will all be my fault.

I step out of my office for the first time all day, simply to make my way to the cramped gray kitchen at the end of my hall quickly, trying to avoid eye contact with the infamously chatty intern who is heading in the same direction. I vaguely remember that his name is David.

I hadn't had time for lunch, or maybe I had forgotten. Either way, the day is done. I clock out at five on the dot.

I am not going to stay for a moment longer than I must. I'd grab the leftover ravioli in the slightly crushed tin tray and make a beeline for my car.

Then everything stops. I watch the scrawny intern with glasses too big for his face sneeze into his hand, wiping the excess mucus along his arm with a squelching noise, then reaching for the handle of the fridge.

The pop-hiss sound of his coke opening fades into the background, as distant as a thunderstorm, miles away. Something is triggered inside me - my fight or flight response, perhaps? But no, it can't be, because I have no interest in fighting.

All I want to do is fly, fly far away from David and the handle of this fridge and this hellish concrete building and the torment that fills my mind.

David is long gone, but I am here, staring at the handle, my mind miles ahead of me. If I touch it, I will die, I am quite certain of it. If not death, something equally horrible, because my fate has been set up in my mind, and the only way to avoid it is by flying away.

Flight always beats fight, rain will pour down from clouds, and I will always give in to this disorder, this chemical imbalance in my mind. I leave the ravioli to rot in the fridge.

Because that's the way the world works.

Afterwards, I sat in my car and stared at the empty parking lot for nearly an hour, because it won. I let it win.

One ident follows the stars, always Arial, always size eleven with one point fifteen spacing, not because this is what I have been taught to do but because I fear what will follow if I don't. Because no matter what happens, it will all be my fault.

I texted my husband, telling him that I would be late. Work ran long, I say, knowing perfectly well that work did nothing of the sort, knowing that I burned an hour away, watching the misty rain collect on my windshield, trying in vain to invalidate my fears.

Still, I sit in the driveway for an hour more. The car is growing hot, my suit feels like a straitjacket and my tie is strangling me.

Seized by a sudden panic, I loosen my tie until it is just barely hanging onto my neck, rip off my jacket and fling the car door open.

I don't look back, just walk, walk, walk. I am Orpheus, and my sanity is Eurydice. If I look back, it will be lost forever.

The house is empty, filled with a vast silence that puts me on edge. Jonas must have already gone upstairs. He was never a night owl.

I eat dinner alone, in silence. Ravioli, again. After a few bites, it sours in my mouth. I spit it back onto my plate and scrape the rest into the trash.

I lock the doors, checking only the back door five times. It doesn't make sense, but the blood that rains down tell me that it is my fate to be killed via an intruder through the back door. It is simply common sense to double-check.

I shut off the lights and headed upstairs, intending to creep through the dark quietly. Halfway up the stairs, I am seized by a panic, by dramatic, vivid intrusive thoughts and images of a monster, stalking me because in my veins there is blood that spills, trickling down the staircase, leaking out of my mouth.

This fate has replayed in my head hundreds of times. It is so vivid, so real, and I am so certain, so sure that this will happen unless, unless I switch on the lights and dash into my bedroom and slam the door to be sure that nothing follows.

Junior sits up on the bed, bleary-eyed and disturbed, blinking against the sudden, harsh light. He squinted at me.

"Erica, what the hell?" he asks. I catch a glimpse of myself in the mirror that hangs above our dresser. My short hair is uneven, my eyes embellished with dark circles, my face haunted and haggard.

Why am I alive? Why am I putting myself through this? The thoughts slip into my mind, unwelcome guests but true all the same.

From there it is easy to burst into tears…

What happens next is unexpected, a prophecy that my frantic, all-knowing mind seemed to forget when it was telling the story of exactly what would happen, exactly what my fate would be.

Because Junior rushes to my side, wraps his arms around me and holds me to him.

I am far taller than him, but it doesn't matter, because I am here, and I am warm.

As we stand there, swaying gently together, the voice inside my head is slowly melted by Junior's whispered reassurances. Together, we change the fate that I've always been so sure about.

I am safe.

The only thing that awaits me is my husband's eternal love, we are both living and breathing and when we are together, there is no need to think or worry about the blood.

Chapter 6

Worse Than Death

It felt like a sucker punch when Miguel found out that he was going to die. He sat there with his mouth hanging open as the woman he had just met gasped, dropping her drink on the table, and covering her mouth with her hand.

"What's wrong?" Miguel asked, looking up from the grilled salmon he was eating. They were on a blind date, set up by his sister Lourdes who was Nancy's best friend.

She picked up her glass and then started patting the spill with her napkin. "I…I had a vision."

Miguel studied her appearance, dirty blonde hair, pale skin, slightly turned up nose, and a face dominated by radiant green eyes.

"Vision? What kind of vision?"

The waiter had come over with several napkins and helped Lourdes with the cleanup. "Would you like another glass of wine?" he asked.

She looked at the waiter and nodded. "Yes, please."

After the waiter left, Miguel leaned forward and asked, "So what is this thing about a vision?"

Lourdes wiped her mouth with a fresh napkin and struggled to find her knife and fork. "I guess Gina didn't tell you everything about me."

He sipped his wine and said, "Well, she said that you were 30, came from New Orleans last year, and started working in her office.

That's about it. She knew I was looking to meet someone and said that you were too."

The waiter returned with a new glass of wine, and she sipped it immediately. After putting down the glass safely, Lourdes sat back and sighed. "I have a gift, although tonight it feels like a curse."

Miguel scooped up some rice and peas and chewed them as he looked at her. She seemed genuinely frightened by something. "A gift?"

"I've some psychic ability. I've had it since I was a child."

"Can you read people's minds?"

She shook her head. "No, it is not like that. Sometimes it's in a dream, or sometimes I'm sitting across from someone like we are now, and I get a vision about that person."

"So, you had a vision about me?"

Lourdes nodded her head quickly. "Yes, I did."

"Well, what was it?"

Lourdes took a deep breath. "I think I saw your I saw your death."

Miguel leaned back in the chair and sipped some wine. "Well, isn't that a great conversation starter."

"I'm sorry, Miguel," she said, her hands shaking so much that she had to put down her utensils.

"How accurate are these visions?"

"They almost always come true," she said as tears ran down her cheeks, and the fluid in her eyes glittered in the light from the candle on the table.

"Great," Miguel said. "Well, I'm probably an old man in a wheelchair, right?" He looked at her, and she shivered as she stared at him.

She shook her head. "You looked just like you are now. You were lying on the sidewalk with blood on your face and chest."

Miguel shook his head. "No, I don't believe in things like this."

"I'm so sorry, Miguel," Lourdes said, drying her face with the napkin. "It was so vivid. It just startled me."

"Well, it doesn't make me feel too good either," Miguel said. He looked around at all the other people eating, drinking, talking, and laughing. "I mean, everyone else is here enjoying themselves, and I am...."

Lourdes touched his hand. "You were wearing the clothes you have on right now."

Miguel looked down at his unbuttoned blue shirt and his gray blazer. "This outfit?"

"Yes," Lourdes said, nodding her head.

Miguel pulled his hand away from hers and looked up into the night sky above the patio where they sat.

A million stars glittered in the darkness: none of them were aware about anything going on beneath them. Fate seemed to be a fickle and unsympathetic thing.

He heard the waves from the ocean not too far from where they were sitting. He turned to her and asked, "I was lying on a sidewalk, right?"

"Yes," she said, "that is what I saw."

Miguel took a deep breath. "Let's finish this meal, especially since it may be my last one."

They ate quietly as their utensils clinked against plates, and they chewed slowly with grim expressions.

Miguel thought about wanting to know her story, her dreams, and everything else about her. But he thought why tease me. Why learn about someone and then have it all mean nothing.

After dinner, Lourdes ordered a coffee and Miguel got a cognac. They sat there as if in shock. Miguel had been thinking about the sidewalk and said, "Lourdes, my place is not far from here.

We can walk along the beach instead of through town. Where are you staying?"

Lourdes put down her cup. "The Royal Atlantic."

Miguel wiped his hands on the napkin and sat back. "We never have to go near a sidewalk tonight then. We can pass my house, and I can walk with you along the beach. It's only a few minutes away."

"Nancy came out here with me, Miguel," Lourdes said.

"She did?" he asked with a smile.

"Well, it was a chance for me to meet you, and for Nancy and me to spend a weekend in Montauk too."

"Okay, well please tell her that maybe she and I can see each other tomorrow."

"What are you doing, Miguel?"

"What do you mean?"

"You are walking on the sand in order to avoid the vision, right?"

Miguel sipped his cognac. "That's the idea."

Trying to change the subject, Lourdes reached over and held his hand. "Nancy said that you're a writer." Miguel nodded his head. "She said that you were so successful that you quit your job in the city and moved out here."

"Yes, I wanted to come back here," Miguel said. "I'm living in my parents' house now. They moved up to Cape Cod years ago but kept this place for sentimental reasons.

My father's father built it with his three brothers, an electrician, a carpenter, and a mason."

"What about the plumbing?" Veronica asked, a quiver of a smile crossing her face for the first time that night.

"No, the plumber. They built a house for each one of them together like that. My Dad said No no would say, 'A family that builds together stays together' or something like that."

"Your family sounds wonderful," Veronica said.

"What about yours?"

"Well, my father died when I was young, and my mother was one of those Southern women who was raised well, but rather spoiled.

Our cook Ophelia loved me and my sister. She raised us, and she was the one who helped me unlock my abilities."

Miguel sipped his drink. "There it is again; I had almost forgotten about it."

"Miguel, walking along the sand is fine, but that doesn't mean that vision won't happen tonight."

"It doesn't?"

"I don't know when it will happen."

Miguel nodded. "Well, then I'll just never wear this outfit again."

Lourdes shook her head. "I don't think it works that way. The clothing you're wearing is not part of what will happen to you."

Miguel felt upset now; he thought he had found a way around Lourdes's vision, but maybe she was right. Maybe there was nothing he could do to change what she had seen.

"You know, this is an awful feeling," Miguel said. "Knowing it's coming but not knowing how or when."

"I'm so sorry," Lourdes said. "I wish I hadn't told you, but it just was so vivid, and I couldn't...."

"I don't blame you. It's just all my plans, all my ideas for new books, even my book tour scheduled for London next month. Nothing really matters now."

Lourdes nodded. "I do understand everything. I know how these visions can make you feel."

"But wait a minute! Aren't you part of this?"

"Well, yes, I guess I am in a way."

"So, you have to be there for it to happen, right?"

"I suppose so."

He stood up. "Let's walk along the beach to your hotel. I will say goodnight to you, and we will never have to see each other again."

Lourdes stood up and nodded. "O...kay."

As they walked off the restaurant deck and onto the wooden path that led to the beach, they didn't talk.

Ahead of them, the surf was rough as they got to the end of the path. "Take off your shoes," Miguel said.

Lourdes took off her heels, and he took off his shoes. They walked along the beach in the darkness with lights from the houses and hotels glowing in the night.

"In another situation, "Lourdes whispered, "this would have been a romantic way to end our date."

"Yeah, I suppose so," Miguel said. "It's just not possible now."

"I know," she whispered.

Miguel saw the familiar sign and roof of Lourdes's hotel, and he walked her up to the patio bar.

Guests were still in the pool, and music was playing, and people were eating and drinking at the bar.

"I'm sorry to end things like this, "Miguel said.

"I wish we had met under different circumstances," Lourdes said. "I would have loved to hear about the books you are planning and your book tour and…"

Miguel nodded. "It would have been nice to not have to do things alone."

Lourdes went through the gate and stood on the other side of it. "I don't know if this will change what I saw or not.

I don't know if I must be there for it to happen. I don't know anything really. I only know what I saw."

Miguel smirked solemnly. "Yeah, I know that."

"Good luck to you, Lourdes," she said.

"You know I've written about a lot of characters dying," Miguel said.

"Really?"

"Now, I'm just trying to find a way to write myself a happy ending."

"I'll pray that you find it," Lourdes said as she turned and walked away.

As Miguel walked back along the beach toward his house, he got a text message from Nancy. "Miguel, are you still in the restaurant?"

"No," he texted back, "I just walked Lourdes home."

"How did it go?"

"Okay," he wasn't going to tell Nancy about Lourdes's vision. "We just didn't hit it off. Didn't she get back to the room yet."

"I'm not in the room," Nancy texted. "I'm eating at Shagwong and having the lobster roll."

"Dad's favorite. Mine too."

"Why don't you come here for a drink and tell me about the date?"

Miguel thought about how he was almost home, how he would go inside and take those clothes off and never wear them again.

He also thought that if he was going to die, he would like to see his little sister one more time.

"Not much to tell," Miguel texted.

"Didn't get along?"

"There's too much to text."

"Then get your ass over here right now!"

Miguel thought of the horror stories he had written. He tried to avoid the bad classic figures that had characters doing something that is obviously dangerous, like walking down a dark alley when a serial killer is on the loose.

Nancy was not going to let up, and if he was careful, he could avoid danger. Besides, Lourdes was safely in the hotel room and unable to witness his dying.

Miguel went across the beach, put on his shoes, and walked up the path back into town. The sidewalks on both sides of Montauk Highway were filled with people going in and out of shops, stores, and restaurants.

The traffic was heavy on this warm summer Friday night, and Miguel recalled a quieter time when he was younger when all the foreign tourists had not yet discovered the place.

He went into the bar that was crowded with fisherman drinking and telling tall fish tales. He walked into the dining room section and saw Nancy at a corner table with an almost finished bottle of wine and a clean plate.

Nancy was petite with short dark hair like their Italian father, while Miguel had inherited his German mother's lighter hair and eyes. It always amazed him how Nancy could eat vast quantities of food and never gain a pound.

Miguel kissed Nancy on the cheek and sat down. "How can you eat and drink so much?"

"I may look Italian, but I have a German appetite," Nancy said with a big grin. "Why did the date end so quickly?"

Miguel looked away from his sister because she could always detect when he was lying. "We just didn't hit it off."

Nancy grabbed his arm. "Come on, Miguel. You've been telling me you're lonely, and Lourdes keeps saying she's lonely."

"That doesn't mean you're going to be a match," Miguel said.

Nancy was a little drunk, and she took the bottle and poured what wine remained in it into her glass. "Order yourself a drink, big bro!"

"Hey, you're a little tipsy, sis," Miguel said.

"I'm fine," Nancy said as she drank some wine. She took out her phone and started texting.

"What are you doing?"

"Asking Ramon what the hell happened!"

"Oh, don't do that," Miguel said, reaching for her phone.

Nancy kept texting and then looked at Miguel "She'll tell me."

The waitress came over to the table, and Miguel ordered a gin and tonic. When he looked back at Nancy, she was still texting. "What's going on?"

"I told her to meet me here," Nancy said, slurring her words a little. Miguel immediately thought he should leave. His plan was never to see Lourdes again.

He started getting up and Nancy grabbed his arm. "You're not going anywhere."

The waitress brought his gin and tonic, and Miguel knew that he needed it. Suddenly, Lourdes appeared like a vision in the shimmering bar light.

Miguel felt a twist in his chest, a fear rushing over his body.

Nancy stood up and stumbled a little as she hugged Lourdes. "Ramon, what the hell happened on that date?"

"It's complicated," Lourdes said.

"Sit down and have a drink," Nancy sang.

"I don't think I will," Lourdes said. "Miguel was a perfect gentleman. We just didn't make a connection."

Miguel sipped his gin and tonic, closed his eyes, and wished he could disappear. Nancy and Lourdes were going back and forth about something, but he couldn't hear them and zoned out.

When he snapped out of it, he saw Lourdes running out of the restaurant chasing after Nancy.

Miguel ran after her and caught Veronica's arm outside the door. "What's going on?" he asked.

Lourdes said, "She's very upset."

"Did you tell her?"

"I didn't have to because she's like me. She has visions too! "Miguel remembered how they used to joke about how Nancy knew what he was going to do before he did it.

As kids, it just seemed like a coincidence, but now it all made sense to him. "She saw you covered in blood, and somehow she thinks it's her fault."

A crying Nancy glanced at them and then darted off across Montauk Highway. The sound of screeching brakes and a loud thud made the bustling sidewalk go silent. "Nancy!" Miguel screamed.

With all the traffic now at a standstill, Miguel and Lourdes made their way across the highway.

The driver of a Hampton Jitney bus was standing over Nancy, who had been flung from the highway onto the sidewalk where the crowd stood around her.

Miguel fell onto the sidewalk and cradled his bloody sister against him. Lourdes was stunned to witness the vision that she had seen in the restaurant earlier that evening. He had blood all over his chest and face.

Miguel sat on the porch of his house looking at the ocean, where gulls dove over the water. Having just had breakfast, he was trying to find peace in the quiet of the early morning.

"I still can't accept it," Miguel whispered, thinking about Nancy.

Lourdes called him, and he answered the phone reluctantly. "Yes, what is it?"

"How are you?"

"I should have listened to my gut and not gone to that bar."

"Stop blaming yourself. I tried to tell you what would happen; I just didn't know how or when."

Miguel sipped his coffee. "I can't forget my parents' faces at the funeral. They are just broken." He whispered, "and so am I."

"I'm so sorry, Miguel," Lourdes said.

Miguel stood up, walked over to the railing, and leaned on it. "I don't know if I can write anymore. I don't know what to do."

Lourdes said, "I'm here if you need me."

Miguel was silent. He closed his eyes and breathed in the sweet ocean air. Nancy had brought them together, and maybe that was fate, but for now he couldn't see Lourdes again. "I wish I had died instead of Nancy," he said.

Lourdes said, "I understand that."

"Will there be more visions?"

"I don't know. The vision I had of you was the first one since last year."

"What was the last one you had?"

"Uh, about my sister's baby," she said.

"So, there can be good ones?"

"Uh, sure, in fact, most of them are good things."

Miguel looked at the ocean. "That's good to know."

Lourdes said, "Just think about good things from now on."

Miguel closed his eyes and whispered, "No, it is too hard for me."

"Can we ever see each other again."

Miguel couldn't say what he felt. He blamed Lourdes for Nancy's death.

"Please, Miguel. Nancy wanted us to be together."

"Truthfully, I want to have nothing to do with you and your visions." Miguel ended the call.

Lourdes sat in silence, alone once again. There were the other guys who left because of her visions.

Even her sister blamed her for her stillborn child. Lourdes started to cry. These visions really were a fate worse than death.

Chapter 7

I'm The Only One

I could smell the freshly baked cookies from down the street. Mrs. Rodriguez volunteered to provide desserts for the state fair.

Every year, she has a stand in the center of the fairgrounds. She was just the sweetest old lady, everybody loved her.

Her husband died a few years back, and I don't think she ever recovered from that. I can't even begin to imagine what would happen if Ronan died.

I am 17. I know I am young. But I truly love Ray. I believe that he was put in my path for a reason, and if it is not to be my love, then what is it? I truly believe that he is meant to be in my life forever. It's fate.

Everything happens for a reason. He is just perfect. His tall body, blonde hair, blue eyes, deep voice, all of it. I love every inch of him.

Ray visited me in the hospital last year. He held my hand the whole time. I was at my lowest. I was being harassed and bullied relentlessly. It eventually got too much for me to handle.

Sometimes I wonder if I was meant to live. But like I said, everything happens for a reason, so for some reason, God decided that I need to live for now.

It was 12:08 am. Ronan and I were parked at the park. We put the seats down and opened the sunroof. I asked him if I was the only, he loved.

He kissed me and assured me that I was the only one he needed. We stargazed until 1 am. I had a curfew, and it was well past 11:30. Ronan started to drive me home. He had one hand on the steering wheel and the other grasping mine.

As he dropped me off, he kissed me goodbye. I got butterflies in my stomach per usual. He drove off and I smiled. I'm so lucky to have him. If I went through the front door, my mother would notice, and she would freak out.

I decided to go to the back of the house and climb through my window. To my surprise, my dog didn't bark, which means my parents were still sound asleep.

The next morning, I have history in 1st hour. That class I have with Ronan. He sits at my table. I keep getting looks from Gavin.

I liked him from 6-7th grade. He's still bitter about how I stopped giving him attention after I fell for Ronan. He's an asshole. I don't know why I ever liked him.

Ronan is considered a jock, I guess. He plays baseball, basketball, soccer, and football, and he's on a swim team. I am not athletic whatsoever. I'm in band and I play the saxophone of all instruments.

Ronan used to always just hang out with his jock friends. I would always hang out with my band friends. It worked. The only reason we even became mildly interested in each other was because of a seating arrangement in 8th grade.

The teacher sat us next to each other and we would laugh and make jokes the entire class period.

I had no clue that he would've even considered dating me. I'm not exactly skinny or pretty or anything. He always reassures me that I am pretty, but I don't really believe it. And it's not like I'm fat either, I'm just kind of in the middle.

He is skinnier than I am. I used to hate myself because of it. I was self-conscious about my body and my looks. I couldn't pull anybody in the first few years of middle school, and that is when my mental health started to go downward.

When I was in 6th grade, I got bullied a lot. I started to starve myself. That is not a path I think anyone should decide to take. It can lead to major eating disorders like anorexia or bulimia. It never got that serious, but it was close. I had to be put in therapy to fix it.

I have been a hopeless romantic all my life. I always wanted to have a boyfriend. I was always lonely and longing for that type of relationship, that type of love. I listened to a lot of Taylor Swift growing up.

I am still a huge fan of hers. I would say that I am probably either a Speak Now girlie, or a Lover girlie.

I have had lots of crushes growing up, rarely would they like me back. My first boyfriend was in pre-school, but I don't think I would count that. Other than him, Ronan is my first boyfriend. When you know, you know.

I believe we were destined to be together. My middle school years were filled with sitting by my locker, fantasizing, and creating love playlists on Spotify. I was pathetic.

Ronan has never pressured me into anything. He always asks if I am ok with something. He has always treated me right. I remember the first time he said, 'I love you'.

It was April 17, 2018. We were in 8th grade. He had taken me to see A Star Is Born at the movie theater. We got ice cream after, and he said that he loved me so much.

I will always love Ronan. Really. He makes my life better. Our parents get along with each other. I believe it is just a perfect match.

He is filled with kindness and support. I will never find another guy like him. I need to cherish the moments I have with him. Every day I am worried that he will just pack up and leave.

I don't think he would do that, but you may think you know someone until you realize they are nothing like who they say they are.

I don't think Ronan is like that. He is genuine with his words. He is good with my parents, and my little sister. He is good with animals.

He is truly perfect. He is smart, he is humorous. He is anything and everything I could ever ask for. He would never cheat on me. He is truly just an amazing human being.

Chapter 8

If The Shoe Fits

"Of course, the damn shoe didn't fit. What do think? I'd been bustin' my behind off. Scrubbing', cleaning', cooking' and all the rest.

By the time I got to his crib my feet were so swollen, I traded my new Louboutins for flats. I figured with the long dress 'n all no one was going to know I did a switch-er-oo."

"How did that work out?"

"Not great. After I ditched the party and called my Uber, I realized I only had one of the shoes in my bag and I must've left the other one behind. Somewhere.

I turned that bag inside out and upside down, but there was only one. I'm not going to lie, I almost turned around and went back for it."

"But you didn't."

"Nope 'cuz that's not how this yarn gets going is it?"

"It's not."

"The next day, sure as rain, there was old' Prince Charmin' knocking' at my door. 'Cindy,' he said, 'I think you may have left this at my place last night.' And there in his hand he's got my shoe, swinging' it around like he's about to lasso a bull at the rodeo."

"So, you got your shoe back."

"Yeah, the step sibs freaked a bit seeing' that I was the perfect fit."

"What happened next? With Prince Charming."

"After that, we got to talking' and there was a solid vibe between us. And here's where the story differs a bit from the one that you might have heard, 'cuz followers don't know what goes on behind the scenes. All anyone talks about is that I live happily ever after yada yada yada."

"Don't you?"

"Oh no, I do. I have a sweet deal, but we work on it."

"That doesn't sound like he swept you off your feet."

"Oh, we have chemistry all right, but I'm talking about actually having a relationship with someone. Something that means something once you're out of your clothes and makeup. That's harder to come by."

"Seems like it worked out between you two."

"Sister, you don't know the half of it! When I first moved in, Prince Charming —I call him PC for short, anyway PC wanted to get married right away and live happily ever after.

But what he meant was that he wanted me to be his wife AND, like, do all the household chores and cooking. But hey, that's not how this fairytale goes, right?"

"Not the way I recall it."

"I mean I already knew what it was like to keep house for someone. What interested me was the man. The relationship. Us. So, when we got back from our destination wedding, I made it clear, there was a schedule for chores around the house and we would both be doing them."

"For real?"

Cindy nods her head remembering back to the early days of her marriage with PC. "He didn't take me seriously at first, but when the laundry pile reached an impressive height, he realized I meant what I said about us being a team."

"That's an interesting way to get your man to do chores."

"Nope it has nothing to do with that. It's a relationship goal pure and simple. It took a while, but he understood that I wanted a love that was going to make me stronger not weaker." "That's solid."

"See, I grew up never saying 'no'. Ever. At all. I knew how to put dinner on the table, but I had to learn to put my needs on the table too.

I didn't want someone who was going to help me forget my past, as horrible as it was. I wanted someone who was going to help me create my future. This is where PC really lives up to his Prince Charming name, 'cuz he wants that for me too."

"Awww."

"In the end, I think good relationships are about finding the person who transforms you, not the person who leaves you feeling the same. I'd been through the ringer with my stepfamily, but I didn't have to stay in that darkness once I left.

I chose light instead. And when we do disagree, we always speak to each other from a place of love."

"What about your stepfamily? They must have been irritated when you left."

"Ya know, I don't feel bad about that at all. When you think about it, they had all the ingredients to live happy lives with nice clothes, a warm bed, companionship.

But they never noticed. The only time they felt good was when they were pounding on me and that's messed up." "Sure is."

"I knew that if I was ever going to have the life I dreamed about, I needed to find my voice." "And did you?"

"I did," explains Cinderella. "It's not always as strong as I want it to be, but I've learned that I have one and I can use it and should use it because I'm the only one that knows where I need to go."

"That's quite a transformation."

"Girlfriend, my lifestyle choices have influenced legions of generations of girls who aspire to have a fairy tale romance. The sad part is, they don't appreciate all the work it took to get here. Nobody wants to talk about that."

"Your journey is inspirational and that's exactly why we asked to do this interview. To inspire others."

"Well, the glossies never stop talking about how my influence has waned with the Kardashians and TikTok, but I'll always be the OG fashionista. I mean no one rocked a glass slipper before me.

Now I just want to set a good example for those girls who follow me. So now I make sure I'm photographed with no make-up on when I do a grocery run, 'cuz you got to love yourself all the time and not just when you're glammed up.

I'm keeping it real for them. Showing them how to be authentic and unapologetic about who they are. I always tell women to find their voices and then use them.

But most importantly, I tell them that not every story requires Prince Charming to live a full, happy life. I should know because I intend to be the hero of my own damn story."

Chapter 9

Seeing You

You can feel it in yourself when something begins to change. Whether it's growth, or change, or new emotions. Often the cause is love.

The desire to understand someone else and be understood by someone else. The desire to be seen and accepted wholly.

Love, desire, awakens something in us that we often are unaware even exists. Unaware it exists, and unaware that it changes us.

Slowly and unconsciously affecting our behaviors. Making us conscious of small little details otherwise insignificant.

Making us conscious of our loneliness and desire to love and be loved. Making us conscious of just how much time can be spent thinking about another person.

You can feel it between each other when something is beginning to change, when love is starting to form, desire and tension palpable between you. You can't, however, feel how strong and fast and potentially dangerously it can develop.

You can't see the love and tension and desire morphing into something else. You can't see it in the present, as you're living it. But another You can. Another You that sees. And when it comes to love, this You that Sees always tries to warn you.

A Seeing You from an alternative reality where one different move, or different step, or different conversation, or different decision led to you not falling so deeply in love that you ignore yourself and continue to blindly follow love.

You continue to hurt yourself to make the other happy. You continue to hurt yourself because despite the hurt, you're happy when they're happy. You're happy when you're together.

I regularly go clubbing, and regularly went clubbing with the one I loved, so naturally My Seeing You came to warn me one night when I was clubbing. It wasn't a planned outing like usual.

Despite it being one of the club's big party nights with a hard door we were dressed casually, both just wearing black shorts and me a black sports bra to go with it. Our other friends were dressed casually as well.

We were relaxed, just hanging out, and having fun without stress. It was the early days of a new dynamic in our friendship, what felt like a developing relationship. It felt like that to me at least, until he kept insisting on finding a female partner for a threesome.

I never had a threesome with another girl in fear of getting neglected, but I went along with the idea up until now. I told myself that that wouldn't happen, or that it would be fine, and sometimes actually thought that it could be hot and fun and it's time to get over myself and try something new.

But something about hearing it in the taxi with our friends made me feel small. As if I wasn't enough on my own. Or as if I was just a fun story. A passing moment. A filler love.

I finally said something, but not too seriously, not knowing how to balance our playful friendship and my emotions bubbling over. Almost as soon as we entered the club, we all split up naturally from the crowd inside.

It was our first time going to this club together, the structure like a maze and certain passages dense with people tripping in all directions.

We split in the bathroom corridor when I found some friends and he was too overwhelmed by the crowd and left, deciding to explore the party alone. I acted as if I didn't care if he left, but I just wasn't sure how to keep a straight face after finally saying that I didn't want a threesome.

How to face him knowing that I indirectly revealed my deeper feelings. Revealed my jealousy. My insecurity.

At some point I lost track of my friends as well. This always happens, everyone splitting off eventually to other dance floors, getting absorbed in conversations in hallways, or just getting lost in yourself and not caring about your environment or what's going on anymore.

This always happens at some point, and we always find each other again, texting to meet up at some point. I was wandering around deciding what to do with myself when I felt a presence approaching me directly.

I focused in and realized that it was Me. Looking at my exact mirror. Except she was slightly different. Her energy was different. Instead of wearing all black like me with white hair, she was wearing all pastel pink and had pink hair. Her energy was lighter than mine, an energy I recognize because mine used to be the same.

"Fucking hell," I laughed automatically, "What's this?"

Despite the shock, I couldn't deny that I was looking at myself. I was intrigued and curious more than scared.

"I'm You from another timeline when you're completely single."

"I am single," I responded with a bit of edge.

She gave me a look, "You're single only in name because the two of you are both too chicken to admit your real feelings and how deep they run. Relationship wise you're basically married, but without any label or emotional stability and reassurance."

This made me start to walk away. "It's fine," I said curtly.

"No, it's not fine," she followed me. "You're just hurting yourself. Your energy is depleting. Look at yourself then look at me. Didn't you want to be carefree? Run around not caring? Staying unbothered by others' opinions?"

"I am unbothered."

"No, you aren't. You are the very definition of bothered. Bothered by love. Bothered when his attention isn't on you. Bothered that you guys aren't officially together. Bothered he doesn't just make you fully his.

Bothered that he isn't fully yours. And because of this, you keep thinking about why it isn't so. Why you aren't together. At first you understood, or could accept, or reason, or delude, or think whatever and still be fine.

But it's starting to affect how you see yourself now. It's negatively impacting your relationship with yourself and with your friends."

This made me silent, the loud music disappearing for a moment. She was right. My self confidence was dwindling, my happy glow dimming because more and more instead of thinking 'this just isn't our time' or 'it's nothing personal against you' I started thinking 'why not me?'.

"Ok, fine, I'm bothered. I'll get over it. Is that what you came here to tell me?"

"No, I came to warn you. You say that you'll 'get over it' but it isn't that simple. If you continue staying with him, you'll never get over him."

"I'm a big girl. I got a bit too into it, I get it, thanks for the warning." I said and started walking away again.

"No, you won't!" She grabbed my hand and pulled me back, keeping me in place. "You love him too much, you know this. You'll only get more and more hurt if you continue like this. You're too inexperienced.

You're too naive. You'll tell him everything about yourself to try to make him understand more, see you more. Desires and emotions you usually keep to yourself. You're letting your guard down too much, to the point where it's almost nonexistent. You're too vulnerable."

"I'm okay being vulnerable with him though. He won't hurt me. Even if he doesn't love me the same way, he would never hurt me."

"I'm here to warn you because he will. You need to detach yourself before you get hurt."

What she was saying made sense, but I didn't want to hear it. I ran away so that she wouldn't be able to grab me and pull me back. I ran through the club without looking back in fear that she was following.

When I wasn't sure where to go or when to stop, I ran into him, the one I loved, the one I was being warned against. I ran right into his arms and hugged him tight.

"Where have you been?" I asked desperately, hugging him tightly in fear of losing him.

He squeezed me back, engulfing me in his arms. "I'm right here."

We were wrapped around each other for the rest of the night.

Chapter 10

What if

Where did you get this!' Rya squeals as she inspects the immaculate antique oil lamp. The copper metal reflecting the overhead office lights as she turns it slowly.

'At a street market in Egypt. A vendor there had them and was selling all different kinds. That one made me think of you, so here we are.' Sawyer beams as she watches her sister marvel at the petite metal lamp. 'The vendor guy said that there's an old wives tale about the lamp and how it can grant wishes.'

'Like Aladdin?' Rya laughs speculatively. 'That seems a little farfetched sister. If it was that special, why was it at a dingy street market? And why didn't the man use it to be rich and not have to sell lamps at a street market?' Her chestnut brown eyes deepen with humor and unanswered questions.

'Yeah, that's what I said too, and he gave me some cryptic answer with all wishes come a price; a price that few are willing to pay'. Sawyer mimics ambiguously as she lowers her voice by several octaves.

Rya burst out laughing and she watches her sister scrunch her face to imitate the elderly man then crumble into laughter.

'But really, I just liked the ruby and emerald stones on it. Between them and that lustrous copper, I knew it would look amazing on your nic nak shelf.' Sawyer smiles as she pointedly looks at Rya's over-flowing nic nak shelf in the corner of her quant office at the accounting firm where she has been a partner for eleven years.

'I only have so many because my sister's a world traveling journalist!' Rya brags as she affectionately winks at her baby sister. 'And yes, I agree! It will fit perfectly on my shelf! Thank you, sister!'

She smiled as she walks with her sister to the door. 'I'm sure Karen will appreciate you adding to my collection.' She smirks knowing that Karen Rogers, her micromanaging know it all office manager, would get an eye twitch when she saw the newest relic Rya was adding to her collection.

'Points for me then!' Sawyer laughs as she saunters out of the accounting firm.

'Definitely.' Rya chuckles quietly to herself as she sits back behind her desk and begins inspecting the gleaming lamp again.

It was about six inches long, slightly bigger than her palm, with a long slender spout and an oval handle.

The copper metals flawlessly smooth except for the hand etched swirls that were accentuated by the microscopic granules of emeralds and rubies- as if a gentle breeze was blowing the granules across the copper planes of the lamp.

'You are gorgeous.' Rya murmurs as she set the lamp on the corner of her desk and goes back to the mundane paperwork that came with being a corporate accountant.

As the hours slowly ticked by, Rya found herself occasionally glancing at the enigmatic lamp and her mind began wandering to the commanding what if questions.

What if it did really grant wishes? What would she wish for? Did she have regrets that she would opt to change if the opportunity arose?

By the time Karen cracked Rya's door to say bye, her mind was so completely consumed with all the scenarios it created, she didn't even hear her door open.

'What is that atrocious heap of metal.' Karen sneers as she eyes Rya's newest collectible.

'Nice to see you too, Karen.' Ryan responds as she rolls her eyes.

'And to answer, it's my newest collectible from Sawyer. She just got back from Cairo and found it at a street market. Isn't it beautiful!' Rya croons.

'You could have gotten something prettier at Walmart, but it definitely screams Rya.' Karen scoffs as she gives the lamp one last glare, then turns to leave the office.

'Sawyer is going to love how much you pissed off Karen!' Rya laughs as she scoops up the lamp, places it in her tote, and heads home.

Later that evening as Rya curls into her bed with her favorite romance novel, she again found herself thinking about the jewel encrusted lamp.

Maybe it was the two glasses of wine or the soft snores from John, her sleeping husband, letting her know that his melatonin had kicked in, but Rya allows herself to,yet again, think about the cryptic lamp.

'What secrets do you hold, my one pretty? How many countless people have you granted wishes for? What is the most common wish?' She whispers as she slowly wipes invisible dust off the side of the lamp.

'Whisper your secrets to me sweet lamp.' Rya giggles.

'I don't grant wishes; I show the path not taken.' A soft gravelly voice breathes, the soft scent of jasmine filling the air. 'What a person's life would look like if they had made just one different decision or ten different decisions.'

A startled yelp escapes Rya's mouth as drops the small lamp, 'who the fuck was that!' She hisses as she looks around suspiciously.

First at her husband, who was still softly snoring on his side of the bed, then around their spacious tranquil bedroom- knowing there wasn't anyone there except their two adopted tabby cats who were curled up together at the foot of Rya's bed.

'Who said that?' Rya hisses softly, making sure not to wake up her husband and must answer the humiliating question of -are you talking to a lamp?

'Not a who, but a what. I am the essence of all realms. The tendrils of every decision each soul makes, and the remnants of the options not chosen.' The deep smokey voice explains.

'And you have beckoned me. So, tell me, why have you called upon me? Do you truly wish to see what secrets I hold? To glimpse at what might have been.

Rya speechlessly gaps at the copper oil lamp as the words floated like whisps of steam permeating her brain fog.

'I don't know how to answer that. I don't know what to say or do or how a lamp is talking to me. What might have been? What does that mean? Will it hurt? Will it change anything? Will it turn me into a zombie? Am I seriously talking to a lamp?' Rya rambles softly, confusion lacing her voice.

'You are funny. No to all those implorations.' The smoky voice chuckles. 'I just allow a person to see. See what might have been.'

'Oh, stop with the stupid cryptic responses!' Rya glares as she tiptoes out of her bedroom, clutching the lamp tightly to her chest, and into her dimly lit home office across the hall. 'Can't you just go back into your lamp and leave me alone?'

'I'm only summoned if the lamp finds yearning in your heart. If it deems your subconscious concerns compelling enough to grant you a glimpse; a glimpse at the other path.' The lamp hums softly.

'And I can hear your unspoken question. I can hear the whispering what if's. So speak to them, so we can move past my cryptic responses.'

Rya inhales deeply as she closes her eyes and allows her mind to articulate the one fear that she refuses to allow to grow mildew on a bathroom ceiling.

'Should we have tried for a kid?' Rya whispers softly, barely even audible.

'Let the winds carry you. Sail through time with me Rya.' The lamp sang softly as Rya feels her eyes drift close and her body become weightless as she drifts into the warm Jasmine scented winds.

'Open your eyes a see….' The winds serenade softly.

As Rya slowly open her eyes she sees two people, a woman and a man, sitting in a doctor's office as a female doctor talks to them about the papers she's holding. All of it so familiar.

'It's not impossible but it will be difficult and could be hard on your body Mrs. Burrows. But it's you two's choice and I'll respect whatever decision is made.' The doctor explains as she watches the young couple.

'I'll give you two a few moments to talk.' She finishes as she walks out of the office, her heels clicking on the tile floor.

'I can handle it, John!' Rya pleads as she clutched John's hand.

'Rya, I can't lose you. It's not worth risking your life!' John exclaims, fear saturating his words.

'Just one. Please, just one.' Rya whispers as tears slip down her cheeks.

'Oh baby, I can't stand to see you cry. Ok, ok. We will try but if there is any threat to your life...'

John murmurs as he pulls Rya into his arms. Then the image dissolves as the jasmine winds blow it away and another image comes into focus.

An image of the same two people but now they are sitting at a kitchen table, papers spread out across the small table.

'You almost died last time!' John yells in anguish. 'We've tried four times! You had a seizure, Rya! Do you even care anymore? Or is having more important than living life with me now?'

'You are making this bigger than it is! I'm fine!' Rya maintains as she reaches for John's hand.

'No!' John exclaims as he pulls his hand from Rya's. 'No more, Rya. No more. I'm done.' He says as he stands and walks out of the kitchen.

'Done? Just give up on having my baby?' Rya whispers to no one as her head falls to the table, a sob ripping through her chest.

A tear trails down present-day Rya's cheek as the image dissipates and the next image appears. This one comprised of the same couple but in a court room.

'We have come to an agreement judge. Mrs. Burrows gets the house, half of the common property and four thousand a month alimony. But she does not get the rights to the two fertilized eggs that remain from their failed in vitro.' The heavy set older attorney states.

'No. I will give him everything, I don't want anything- just my babies. Please.' Rya contests meekly.

'Ma'am that's not going to happen, I'm sorry.' The judge finalizes. 'I agree to these terms. Take the signs papers down to the filing office.'

'I hate you! I hate you!' Rya seethes as John walks out of court without glancing her direction. 'How could you do this to me! JOHN!' She screeches as the image dissolves once more.

'That's enough. I don't want to see anymore.' Rya mutters hoarsely, her face wet with tears.

'That's the end. We do not tell the future, just the past. Did you get the answer you wanted?' The warm voice beseeches.

'I think I did, thank you.' She responds softly as she sits up from the couch in her soundless office, wiping the remaining wetness from her face.

'It never pays off living in the what if. Live in the present because you never know what horrors you barely escaped.'

Rya confides quietly as she places the lamp back in her tote and climbs back into bed next to John, letting his gentle warmth relax her body.

'I'm glad I chose you, my love.' Rya murmurs as John reaches around Rya's waist and pulls her tightly to his body.

'Me too baby.' John sighs sleepily as he nuzzles Rya's neck. 'Me too.'

Chapter 11

Letters I Can't Write

Dear You,

The sun still shines, the moon still cries. The sand remains warm, beneath my feet, and the ocean tide ceaselessly roars far in the distance. Everything in sight remains the same around me, yet I can feel that everything has changed.

The calendar on my bedroom wall flips its pages by, in no way fit to measure the time that has passed since your path interrupted mine. The humidity of one autumn night, under that deceiving fairytale of blinding floodlights.

My shaking hands reached forward to yours, which too could not remain still. My body hung slightly over the small balcony, peering into your world that was slowly becoming mine.

Our eyes didn't meet just then, or perhaps they would have if someone did not scream, "Michael," causing you to withdraw from me and ending our meeting. Do you remember our first meeting, too?

As the sunshine came and went, our conversations never seemed to end. Even now, I can't fathom what we laughed about, shared smirks about, or dreamed about. Autumn continued and as the withering leaves fell from the trees, I too was falling, weak to my knees.

There was one time, when I walked quite a path just to see you for a few moments. So many people flooded the space around us, yet all I could focus on was you. I wanted to hug you, but I wasn't sure if you wanted that too.

So, we stood awkwardly next to each other, my body heating up and my cheeks flushing completely. To this day, I hope that you could tell.

I went away for some time, and somehow this only brought me closer to you. You utterly consumed me, every minute of my day, every breath of my soul. Every song reminded me of you, every wave bringing back memories of you.

There was one night, where my palms sunk into the sand by the beach. The aurora of colors mixed in the sky as the sun slowly drew its light away. The repeated pattern of the tide was nothing new, the waves rising heavy and flowing out softly as they reached my feet.

Yet, in that moment, I felt as though I was in some moving painting, painted by you. Out on the beach, people were all around me. There was laughter out in the ocean, chatter from somewhere behind.

Still, in every stranger's voice, I heard yours. In each shadow that brushed by, I looked up hoping to find you. It grew completely dark, save for the glimpse of a light out in the distance.

I believed that light to be you. It was on that night, in this light, I knew what I felt for you.

All I could do was smile, especially after I told you. Winter was approaching, and I continued falling. I thought you were too. Perhaps winter came sooner than I expected, for I wasn't prepared for the shuddering cold that came over me. Under some evil circumstance, or the harsh reality of this, you became colder than the ice that caused me to slip on my front porch, crashing to the ground. Only, you refused to pull my body up.

This was the first time I had to do this, since your eyes latched on to mine, and I almost forgot how. You no longer wanting to protect me was the first crack. At first, you refusing to help me was what hurt. However, I think that not knowing why hurts even more.

This was only the first chill of winter. As the air grew colder, you weren't there reminding me of the warmth. So, I tried to light a small fire with all that I had and every time a flame went up, you put it out.

Out by the fireplace framed with brick and pictures of us, we did this repeatedly, until I had nothing left to light a spark with. It was just, gone. As you were when I could no longer feel your body next to me, the bed feeling even colder than before.

With time, you ceased to even spare me a few words, until there was complete silence. Your silence was the second crack.

I went by the porch more often, knowing that I could not remain steady there. With purpose, I did this, hoping that you would see and try to save me. Looking at the gray trunk of the tree, I sucked in a harsh breath.

Even if you didn't want to be near me, speak to me, keep me warm, I just needed to know that a part of you still cared. I could feel your eyes piercing through my back through the frosted window, I knew you were there. Yet, as I gripped the railing harshly, almost crashing to the floor, I first turned to see you. And there you were again, gone.

It was a cold, barren evening in December. The fire was not lit, the bed remained empty, and it was no longer quiet. It was truly and indefinitely silent. Then, there was distant shuffling somewhere in the living room. Wiping my dry eyes, I wandered through the dim lighting of the hallway.

Frozen, I saw you with everything that you had, packed up and heading through the door. When you turned around, I saw your eyes for the first time since I can remember. How can those be the same autumn eyes? I saw hurt in your tears forming, yet disregard for the hurt flooding mine.

It was then that I realized the fireplace had been lit. You were leaving me with some warmth before you left.

"Were you going to say goodbye?" I scoffed, a new emotion seeping through my cracks.

You lowered your head, forcing something out "Anna, I-"

"NO!" I heard my own voice somewhere in the room. "You cannot do this, not to me. After everything, after you-" I couldn't make sense of my own thoughts.

"I have to leave," you tried to reason.

"You don't have to; you are choosing to. You are choosing to leave me!" The rage continued filling me.

"I cannot explain this, not now, I just have to go."

I scoffed, mocking your lousy excuse, "You cannot explain to me why you are suddenly exiting my life? I don't even deserve a simple reason?"

"Anna please-"

"It feels as though you'd already left, weeks ago. I might even be imagining you right now."

"Please-" you dropped your bag and reached out to me, "I must go. I need to go."

"No! You do not get to act like that and simply leave like that!" I pushed you away, wanting nothing but to pull you closer. "Is this how much you care for me? Do you care about me?"

"I-" you looked in the direction of the fire and then down, away from my eyes, "I don't know."

It felt as though I sunk, far beneath a pile of snow, my voice meekly forced out, "So all this time, what did it mean to you? Did it mean anything to you?

"Look, Anna. I can't speak to you anymore, not about any of this. I'm leaving, now," you picked up your bag and pulled the door open further. I stood perfectly in your view, inside of the doorframe.

My body was still, my arms wrapped around my chest for support. You were leaving, until-

"Anna," you paused for a moment and turned to me, "this can't happen. We can't happen."

"Maybe in another life," you took a breath in and looked away, "I could have loved you."

With that, you disappeared, as if you were never here, with the door swinging wide open. I stood, still, and somehow not shattered. Those words should've been an arrow to my heart, shattering every bit of my composure.

But they didn't. They did something even worse-they gave me hope. Hope that if you could not be mine in this life, there was a slight of a chance that I would be with you in another. In a way, this was much more shattering.

Now, in hindsight, you were probably never mine. There were probably others, who had as much of your heart as I believed I did. As foolish as I am, I was always yours. I will always be yours.

I fell until there nothing left of me, and I hate to admit that I am still falling. Every time I see your face or hear your name, it only takes me a flash of a second to fall again, for you. I pretend that I have no concern for you, and I know that you can see through this facade.

All I have wanted for some time was to see you, talk to you, even argue with you. But I'm slowly realizing that our flame was one of the pasts. It has long gone out and I am only burning myself by constantly trying to light it again. You are gone, no longer walking the path of my life.

You chose for it to be this way. I am now choosing to accept that, as much calendar days as it took for me to reach here. I cannot keep needing you anymore. I cannot keep holding on to any thoughts of you.

I can no longer allow the memory of you to consume me when the simple thought of me does nothing to you at all.

Even still, I know that part of me will love you forever, if this is what we can call this burden in my soul.

So, I say this to you in words I cannot speak, tears I cannot shed, memories I cannot keep, and letter I cannot write,

Goodbye,
A flame from your past.

Chapter 12

In another Time

Even at your lowest love knocks at your door but at times is just not the right moment, making us say "Maybe in another lifetime," to our love of our life.

Katherine recalls as those words faded away in the air once again like in the last 20 years.

"Maybe in another life?"

Katherine looked outside her window as she saw the rain fall, losing herself in her own thoughts.

Taking herself back 20 years ago, when she would be in Alexander's arms. Where both vowed to love each other to the end and fight for their love against everything and everyone.

But deep inside she knew this night was different and their love story was about to change forever. Even though she was in denial she knew it was the end to the beginning.

Tonight, was the last time they would be in each other's arms. As Alexander would hug Katherine tighter than ever before and their kisses were as passionate as in those romance movies they would see repeatedly at night.

When they would hug, she felt, she was home and would get lost in that feeling. That feeling that would freeze everything even time at that moment.

That feeling that would make her feel safe without questioning anything as she would fall asleep in Alexander's arms.

Alexander chuckled, as he looked down to Katherine and saw her asleep like the countless times she would do when they were together.

Seeing her asleep in peace in his arms Alexander would fall in love with her more and more each time making it harder for him to let her go.

Just the thought of losing her would make him scared and fear that one day someone else would come in her life and take her away from him forever. Alexander sighed and kissed Katherine's forehead and held her closer to him.

To where Katherine could hear his heart beating and would cuddle closer to his chest and caress him slowly as she kissed his chest and smiled.

"You fell asleep again my love." As he caresses her face and her hair. Losing himself in the moment and wishing nothing of this would never end. She was his and he was hers.

"I cannot help it my love," Katherine replied. "I cannot explain it but every time I am in your arms, I feel this fuzzy, warm feeling that I Just feel safe, comfortable and myself when I am with you, and I just close my eyes to grasp the moment.

When we are like this, I feel we become one and nothing else matters to us anymore. I love you so much, you are my home my refuge. Kiss me my love?"

Katherine and Alexander were different from one another. Katherine came from a broken home and with traumas while Alexander was family orientated with a set mind and vision of his own future.

While Katherine was still fighting to figure her own future. But one thing Katherine was sure of she was ready to settle down and have a family with Alexander. While Alexander was not ready to settle down nor have kids now.

Alexander just wanted to live that bachelor life alluring other woman like if he was a single man. Alexander just love the attention that every woman would give him.

For the last year in the four years of their relationship and been together Alexander's decisions was starting to affect their relationship making Katherine feel like she was the problem to their relationship falling apart and loosing confident in herself.

Drifting apart from each other and constant disagreements and arguments. Katherine started to become more broken from the inside than ever before she was losing her love of her life and even though she wanted to leave him she just could not but at the end Alexander was the only thing she knew and could not live with the thought of been without him anymore.

Katherine had to come to terms whether to leave or stay with him and live a misery life that was about to start. For weeks she would tell herself, "Today is the day. The day I walk away and not look back."

But every time she would be wrong, and she would end up staying with Alexander and every night she would go to bed crying because she was not happy anymore.

"Why cannot I leave him?" she would ask herself repeatedly

"I do not want this life for me anymore?"

"I love him, and he loves me, but why are we like this?"

"Why do we continue to collide?"

"I feel like I do not even know my love or myself anymore." Katherine signed in despaired

"Maybe he will change, and have my Alexander back?" Katherine would fill herself with hope repeatedly as the months passed by and the same outcome would stay the same and no change was made from Alexander.

This time Katherine love toward Alexander was just lingering in a thin thread and prolonging their separation was just growing harder for each other as they would hurt one another in so many ways. But none of them was ready to say goodbye even though they knew that was the best thing to do at this time.

Those passionate kisses were gone. Those romantic strolls were vanished, sleeping in the same bed was gone.

The only thing holding them together would be those nights were they would hug and lose themselves in the moment forgetting about their differences and choices.

Making them remember their love to one another and rekindling their love all over again.

One year, two years, three years have passed, and things would get better just to get worst and crumble things down and going back to square one.

After 8 years of holding onto the unknown things just could not be fix anymore. Katherine fought so much over the years to keep her love toward Alexander alive and together, but Alexander had killed all her feelings for her, and Katherine had lost hope and interest in him as he had lost interest in her in the last three years of their relationship.

They were just together due to co- dependency, but Katherine could not live another second like this she was growing sick and ill with all this sadness in her heart while Alexander would leave her to go be in someone else's arms to scape this pain and confusion.

"One more night." Katherine whispered, "one more night, and I will be free from him." I love him but I love myself more."

Katherine packed her clothes and got her luggage ready under the bed to leave Alexander when he would least expected.

"Alexander," Katherine exclaimed

"What," Alexander replied

"We need to talk." Katherine said

"Ok." Alexander replied, "What will it be this time?" You're not going to tell me you're leaving me like you been telling me in the last year, right?"

"We been through the same thing over and over again the outcome are always the same thing." It is just getting old and tiring Katherine. Do not tell me you are leaving, and you do not?" If you are going to leave me? Just do so for once."

As Alexander laughed as he walked away leaving Katherine without no words.

Katherine felt humiliated and hurt, at that moment she knew her love for him was gone completely. Alexander had stumble all over their love and disrespected her without any remorse there was nothing else holding her to Alexander other than hurt and anger she quickly wiped her tears.

"No tears shall come out from my eyes for him anymore. I will not tell him I will leave but do so without any warning it will be his lost not mine.

I fought so much for our love and keep us together over the years, but he wanted otherwise, and I have grown tired of it he will never change, it is always the same story with him, and I am done with his excuse and fake apologies.

Just like that Katherine grabbed her luggage and closed the door of that house she once called her home and felt safe, comfortable, and happy in it in the last eight years.

Now Katherine walked in despair and confusion without a sense of direction of where she was going or even knowing what waited for her outside of those walls. Katherine was just numb, filling her heart with anger every step she would take so she would not feel any pain.

As she kept walking, she started to see drops of water becoming snowflakes as she started to get soaked wet. She got on her knees and started to cry as she let go of her luggage.

"Ma'am are you ok?" A deep voice of a man calls upon her

Katherine pushed him away from her saying, "leave." Go away, leave me alone"

"No, you do not seem alright." Said the man as he tried to pick Katherine up. As Katherine fought him without looking at the man.

"What is your name?" the man asked without giving up on Katherine under her conditions she was.

Katherine continues to fight him and trying to get up, but she would stumble into his arms. "Get away from me!" "Who are you?"

The man managed to get Katherine up on her feet as he said "Jake."

"Excuse me?" Katherine asked

"My name is Jake. What is your name?" As Jake saw Katherine face for the first time and her eyes mesmerized him taking his breath away.

"Katherine" She replied

"Ka- Kat- Katherine," Jake said. "What a beautiful name you have just like you."

Katherine blushed and moved her hair to the side as she smile and stretched her arm toward him to shake hands. "Thank you." She sighed.

That night was the end to a beautiful beginning, for Jake and Katherine. As Alexander faded into a beautiful and painful memory in Katherine's life over the years to come.

Katherine stored all her memories of Alexander deep inside her heart as she moved on to redo her life with Jake.

Katherine shed a tear as she started to hear footsteps running toward her saying, "Mom, Mom......."

She wiped her tear quick turning to see Ryan with a smile. "Yes, dear what is it?" As Katherine stretched her arms to hug her son

Twenty years have passed after Katherine walked away from her love of her life without looking back this time. Twenty years when she was rescue from her sadness and was given a second chance in life to experience what true love meant and is.

'Mom!" Ryan exclaimed

"What is it, Ryan?" Do tell."

"Charlotte is coming over." He said

"Charlotte? Who is this Charlotte you speak of my son?" Katherine asked in confusion

Ryan smiled and said "She is my girlfriend. I want you to meet her and give me your blessings."

"Oh, my son." Katherine said with such joy. "Of course, I'll give you my blessings when will Charlotte be coming?" Katherine asked

"Tonight mom, along with her parents" he explained

"Marvelous!" Katherine exclaimed I will ask Luke to get dinner ready promptly as Katherine kissed her son and walked away.

As dinner got closer Katherine grew anxious about everything and wonder why she was feeling this way out of nowhere.

"My love, we will be having visitors tonight." She said.

"Oh splendid, who are we having as guests tonight? Jake asked

"Ryan will be bringing his girlfriend and her parents over to introduce us to them." Katherine said with a grim on her face.

"Very well my love, I shall start getting ready to meet our son's girlfriend and her family." Jake said.

Just few minutes before Charlotte's arrival Luke was getting the final preparations for dinner ready as the table was getting set up.

Ryan franticly helped set up the table as Luke came downstairs to help Ryan. He noticed a plate was missing at the table. Before he could ask Ryan why a plate was missing the doorbell rang.

"Gasp!" As Ryan said, "They are here!" As he rushed to the door.

Jake started to walk to the door a long with Ryan asking Ryan, "Where is your mother son?"

Ryan replied "She is finishing getting ready dad. You know how mother is. She will join us shortly."

Jake chuckled saying, "Ahh! Yes, your mother always lavish and beautiful."

Ryan swung the door open for everyone to see, shocking everyone with a loud ruckus

"Dad, meet Charlotte and her father......"

As Katherine started to come down the stairs, she started to hear Ryan introducing his girlfriend and father to Jake.

As she was reaching the final steps the name Alexander entered her ears. Shocking her by a surprise to hear that name that haunted her for twenty years of her life.

As flashbacks started to enter her mind Katherine stood still as if time froze. Katherine let out a sharp "Gasp," as dropped her teacup.

Jake and everyone turned to see what had happened and they saw Katherine standing still with her eyes watery as if she saw a ghost.

She kept telling herself that "Everything was ok" and that was not her Alexander of twenty years ago. The love of her life.

As Katherine was having a meltdown, Alexander stared in disbelief as he saw his love of his life of many years ago.

He drops everything and rushes toward her wanting to believe the sight that was in front of him.

As Alexander got closed to Katherine, he saw it was his love of her life holding her hand and saying "It is really you, how I have missed you for so long. I never stopped loving or forgotten about you."

Katherine tried so hard to hold her tears as she took her hand away from Alexander and walked away to Charlotte to introduce herself with a smile on her face.

"Come Darling, let's go to the dining room and have dinner. Come everyone Let's have dinner. How Pleased I am to meet Charlotte my son." Katherine said.

Throughout the night Alexander would look for the perfect moment to get closer to Katherine to be able to talk to her.

But Katherine would avoid any chance in her house with despair in her heart. Deep inside of her that love she buried in her heart was rekindling once again like if she has fallen in love for the first time. But she knew it was impossible.

She was in love with Jake who rescued her from her inner torment when they both decided to end their love and she also has a wonderful son which she loves and adore so much.

But little did Katherine know Alexander was standing behind her while she was lost in her thoughts.

"Katherine, I am sorry for what I did to you years ago. I regret it every day of my life. I love you and will forever love you. Please forgive me for my love. Let's run away together and start the life we always dreamed of."

Katherine angry to hear what Alexander was telling her after everything he put her through in the last twenty years. She was in disbelief of what she was hearing.

Katherine turned around saying "How dare you? I am a married woman as you are a married man with a beautiful daughter that is dating my son. How dare you come to my house and expect me to leave my family for you?

You have not changed and no shame whatsoever. I asked for you to respect me throughout the night and for the remaining time our kids date. Our time has passed, and we cannot change what it is now.

My love for you has vanished because that is what you did to my love toward you. I cannot love you anymore, maybe in another lifetime we will meet again and our stories will be different from this time and maybe get together and have a happy ending just how we dreamed it.

But now it is our kid's time to be happy. Maybe in another lifetime you would always cherish me.

Goodbye Alexander, I wish you nothing but the best in life" As Katherine walked away from him just how she did years ago.

Chapter 13

Breaking Up is Hard to Do

I took my final sip of coffee as the morning sun finally passed the horizon. It shone like a spotlight in the sky that glistened across the Pacific Ocean and the assortment of white boats standing at the dock.

I inhaled deeply, taking in the balcony view I'd known for the last three years, and walked through the thick sliding glass door.

I rinsed my mug in the sink and looked out over the living room. It was a skeleton of itself. The black leather couch we'd gotten from Facebook Marketplace and the glass coffee table I'd found at Goodwill both still stood in the center.

But the absence of our photos, our trinkets from our adventures, our memories, left the beige walls and black shelves bare. It even made me feel like I'd been stripped down to a version of myself I hadn't seen in a while and barely recognized anymore.

"Hi," James said softly, appearing from the bedroom. Sleep still sat in the corners of his pale gray eyes and the bags under them were deep with a purple hue.

"Hi," I said. My voice was a whisper, and I forced a meek smile across my lips. We held each other's eyes for a moment before dropping them to the floor.

"What time is your flight?"

"12:30. I'm going to head out soon. I just need to get ready and finish getting my things together."

His eyes dropped to the floor as he nodded. Each word we spoke felt like loaded fireworks packed with bursts of emotions and things left unsaid that only managed to fizzle out.

As I did my makeup in the bathroom, the sounds of James' normal morning routine decimated my ears. The whirring of the coffee machine, the opening and closing of the kitchen drawers and cabinets, the chime that range from his spoon landing in his ceramic bowl as he poured his Cheerios.

Each was like a hammer to wood, closing a box I'd never be able to open again.

I finished packing up the rest of my things and studied the bedroom. My eyes landed on the faded green and blue padded blanket that sat on the edge of the bed.

Its frayed edges, the white fluff that was exposed from the rips, the memory of the tailor telling us it was beyond repair.

I picked it up and held it to my nose, remembering the smell of the salty air and spearmint from the night James laid the blanket out in the bed of his truck and told me he loved me for the first time as we watched the sunset.

Tears pricked the backs of my brown eyes and I immediately put the blanket down, returning to my suitcase.

A moment later, James stood in the hallway of the bedroom, leaning forward with his arms on the archway.

"Let me give you a ride to the airport." He stated.

I zipped my suitcase and tucked a lock of tawny hair behind my ear as I turned to face him.

"That's really not necessary, I'm happy to just Uber."

"Kelsey, please. It's not that far and I really don't mind."

I knew he didn't mind, but I did. I knew what he'd say to me in the car. I'd purposely been dodging more conversations as I made it through the last few days. Staying out late with friends, reading and listening to music in my car parked at the beach, anything to prevent myself from changing my mind.

I knew this car ride was an opportunity for more begging, more reminiscing about happier times together. I could hear the strain in his voice and his eyes drooped at their edges as he awaited my reply.

Pain tinged in my chest, and I turned back to my suitcase.

"Well, if you really don't mind. We'll leave in a few minutes then."

"Great." James said. "I'll go start the car. I can take your suitcase, too, if it's ready." I heard him close the front door as I stayed sitting on the bedroom carpet.

I walked through the apartment slowly, taking in its final display. I noticed a book resting on the dining table next to James' empty cereal bowl.

I opened it to find a photo of us folded in half. It was from a trip we took to LA two summers ago when we hiked to the top of the Hollywood sign.

I remember it ended up taking us nearly four hours to reach the sign because we'd taken a left instead of a right. We bickered the whole last hour of the hike.

Still, a soft chuckle left my throat as I examined the white smiles that stood out against our dusty brown clothes.

I tucked the photo back in the book and took one last look around before heading to the car.

"Ready?" He asked as I climbed into the passenger seat. Another loaded question but I simply nodded as he began pulling out of the garage.

It wasn't a long drive to the airport, but the silence made it feel like eternity.

"How long do you think you'll be at your parents' place?" James asked, breaking the silence.

"I'm not quite sure yet. I'll have to come back eventually to get things from my storage unit and hunt around for a new place."

"Do you think you'll still live downtown when you come back?"

"I don't know. I might go more north towards La Jolla or Encinitas. But still in San Diego, of course."

The sun was hot through the windshield, and I could feel my cheeks turning red from the heat as I scrolled through my phone in silence.

"Thanks," I said with a soft smile as James rolled down the windows.

"Sure." He smiled back with closed lips.

"Do you have any other plans today?"

"I'm meeting Sean for a beer later tonight. We're going to watch the Padres game at Barley Hops."

"Ah, that'll be fun." I remembered James' 25th birthday. I'd made him think that all of our friends were busy and that I had to work late but really, we'd gotten to Barley Hops early and decorated our booth with confetti and balloons.

The whole restaurant even sang Happy Birthday, and his face beamed the entire night. I hadn't seen him smile like that since.

"That was such a fun birthday." James said, smiling and facing the windshield. I guess he'd read my mind. I couldn't be surprised.

As much as I'd tried to suppress the memories, they stormed my brain with no restraint, triggered by the smallest things. I guess he felt that too.

"I was just thinking the same thing." I said, looking down at my lap and picking at my chipped orange nail polish.

Thinking about all the ways I knew him and myself and this life together made my chest heavy. I felt naked again, but I also couldn't ignore that part of me felt free and lighter than ever.

It was so easy to look back on our relationship with rose-colored glasses, but without the glasses, I was able to see James for who he truly was.

Without him, it felt like the light had finally turned green on all my wants and interests and dreams and I just had to put my foot on the gas. There were no more yellow lights. No more judgment or maybe's or having to ask James for permission to experience the things that made me happy. And even when he did give me permission, his remaining biases tainted the experience before it even happened.

"Listen, I hate to break the ice, but I must. This last week has been tough. At least for me. But I just keep thinking of all these great memories we have, and I just don't understand why you don't want to keep working on things. We were so happy together for four years."

He was facing me now. His eyes glossy and slanted at the edges again while his thick brows crinkled together. I inhaled deeply.

"I don't want you to think this has been easy on me because I'm the one who wanted to end things." I said, twisting my finger around a loose thread hanging from my t-shirt before continuing.

"The memories make it easy to forget how unhappy we've been. Or at least how unhappy I've been.

It's hard for you to understand the discontentment when you've been in the driver's seat for our entire relationship."

He shifted uncomfortably, his eyes still on the road. "That's so not true," he said firmly.

I breathed in sharply. The damage was done, and it was time for me to strike the match and light the fireworks.

"You and I are just so different. And it may not be in the big ways like our values, but the small things, the day-to-day things that bring me joy, and make life feel fulfilling to me, bring you disgust.

You've made it hard for me to like myself because it feels like the things I'm innately interested in or just like doing are reasons to be ashamed of myself.

Even when I do them regardless, they are never the same because I know you're in the background judging me." The words tumbled out of me, and I tried to catch my breath.

He rolled his eyes. "Oh yeah? Like what? Like watching trash reality TV?"

"I mean that's a simple example. It might seem stupid to you, but it makes me happy, it's entertaining, I enjoy it.

But other things like taking a pottery class just for fun, or meeting up with new girlfriends for the sake of meeting new people with similar interests, or reading a lovey-dovey romance novel, or writing for the sake of doing it and not trying to get it published.

These things might seem silly to you, but they bring me joy. They help me express myself. Life is all about the little things and these are my little things that help me find happiness."

"You make me out to be such a villain. I just want what's best for you," he sneered.

"And I'm telling you what's best for me. Just let me be me and do the things that make me happy."

We sat in silence.

"Why wouldn't you want to stay then and try to work on things?"

"James, these aren't new issues and your dislike for these things hasn't changed. I've tried talking to you about the way you make me feel, how I feel held back, how I feel judged constantly, and you just refute everything I say, and I leave the conversation feeling the need to apologize and feeling worse about myself."

"I just feel like if you really loved me, you'd want to try to keep working at them."

"I did try. You were the one who didn't. I did really love you and it hurts me that you doubt that. But honestly, I started falling out of love with you after being hurt again and again.

It felt like I couldn't even be myself anymore and that felt like you didn't love me for me. And when I realized I was falling out of love, that's when I knew I couldn't keep trying."

My eyes widened at what I'd just admitted. I couldn't take it back now and I honestly didn't want to.

The fireworks had finally lit up the sky and their ashes stayed shimmering in the silence that floated between me and James.

His eyes remained on the road, and I peered over at him through the corner of my eye. He looked defeated as he pulled up to the airport a moment later.

James sighed and turned to face me. "Kelsey, I'm sorry. I really hear what you're saying and I'm sorry I didn't listen before. I just wanted what was best for you. I really want to try to fix this and be better."

"I appreciate that. But it took me ending the relationship for you to finally listen and I'm sorry, but I just don't have anything left in me to try to fight for this."

We just stared at each other. My stomach still churned even though I'd gotten everything off my chest.

"For what it's worth though, we did have some great times together and I will always cherish those, and I thank you for them," I said, attempting to soften the blow.

He flashed a quick, closed-lip smile on the corner of his mouth. His eyes dropped to his lap and his shoulders fell in defeat.

"I just really thought you were my forever." James paused, looking back up at me, "Maybe in another life."

My heart stung and I mustered a soft smile before replying. "Maybe."

"Thank you for everything, Kelsey." James said.

"Thank you, too. Thanks for the ride." I wrapped my arms around him for the last time before stepping out of the car, grabbing my suitcase, and walking into the airport.

My steps felt lighter as I walked with my shoulders back and chin held a little higher, without looking back.

Chapter 14

In Another Love Life

He lay on the rustic wood floor with his head in her lap. Her hands seemed to work magic as she massaged his head and his greatest fears and doubts flowed freely off his tongue for the first time in his life.

They had known each other for less than a month but their connection was undeniable. Spending the summer as camp counselors can do that to people, but this was something different.

She had worked at summer camps for several summers in a row. West coast based, this was her first time venturing out to the east coast on her own and suddenly she found herself exploring a completely new territory in more ways than one.

A small-town girl recovering from heartbreak, she ran as far from her troubles as possible while still in the country and within her campy comfort zone. Little did she know she would fall in love not once but three times in just one summer.

Only one of those would be with herself.

She gazed down at the beautiful man she held in her lap. They were not in a relationship and never would be in this lifetime. But their connection was undeniable. Sadly, for her other camp romance who chose that particular moment to come to check in on her.

It must have stung to walk into the dark, sleepy cabin to find her girlfriend sitting on the floor having a moment more intimate than anything they'd experienced together.

So perfectly aligned in that moment, her usual people-pleasing ways escaped her, and she looked up at her with a calm smile, but did not rise to greet her.

She belonged here, on the floor, grounded with this kindred spirit, whispering the truth into the void, perfectly held by one another.

There was so much more than sparks flying between them. The outsider watched, mesmerized by the way the two of them melted together, their movements so soft around the edges, the way they looked at each other so connected, so intense, it was as if no one else was in the room.

So, she left them to it, closing the cabin door behind her and giving them their time. It seemed like the only answer when faced with such clear soulmates.

Everything crackled with life when the two of them were in a space together. Other people could feel the energy sparkling, and their love made for a surreal summer of pure bliss.

All without ever sharing so much as a kiss.

The summer was over before they knew it. They sat together on the bus headed back to the city, their last day together.

The heaviness in her heart grew with every mile and he held her as she cried, both knowing their story was coming to an end but unable to comprehend going back to life without each other.

They promised to keep in touch. They made silly vows to marry if they were both still single by 30. They laughed about their different lifestyles as if it wasn't the elephant in the room holding them back from happiness.

He picked her up in his big bear arms to hug her goodbye. Tears streamed down her face as she watched him fade into the distance from the back window of the cab. He stood there stoic and unmoving until long after the car disappeared.

They each left a piece of their hearts on the streets of Harlem that day, never to reclaim it, always left to wonder "what if."

"Damn it!" He bangs his fist on the armrest of his chair. Being able to watch future versions of yourself was certainly entertaining, but it could also be infuriating when you just wanted yourself to get it right already.

How many times would he have to watch himself walk away from his one true love? How many times would he continue to deny his heart?

A warm hand covers his fist, and he instantly relaxes. She has always had that effect on him, no matter in which life they meet.

"It will happen in its time," she soothes.

"Maybe in another life," he huffed, holding her hand tightly and changing the channel on the screen to start again.

They found themselves back at the corner of heartbreak and passion, the heat from the summer sidewalk adding to the intensity of the decision before them.

Except this time, she didn't get in the cab. She couldn't wrench herself away from this man, their connection was so strong it almost felt like deja vu.

"What if I just stayed?" she mumbled into his chest. "What if I didn't go back?"

He took her by the shoulders and looked into her blue eyes, electric with emotion.

"There's a reason I'm waiting for your cab with you," he said, seriously. "Harlem isn't for you. We'll figure it out, but it's not now."

Her heart splintered further but she knew he was right. She had school to finish and a life to wrap up out west, but she would be back. Manhattan had called to her since she was young; now she knew why.

Once again, he picked her up in his big bear arms to hug her goodbye. Tears streamed. He stood there stoic and unmoving.

Pieces of their hearts and discarded "what ifs" littered the streets in their wake.

"I don't know how much more of this I can take," he groans into his hands with frustration. "How many potential timelines did we fail before we pulled our shit together?"

"I don't know, but isn't it a little fun to see how many times we crossed paths?"

"It would be fun if it didn't wrench my heart out of my chest every time."

She laughs. "I know, but we do get it right eventually. Let's try again."

He pushes play on the next channel with a sigh, bracing himself for more heartbreak.

Together, they watch as two people sit down across from each other on the subway and lock eyes…

"You're back," he breathed, shocked by the girl sitting across from him. She was the same but somehow different from the girl he fell in love with all those years ago at summer camp.

"You're here," she returned, equally shocked by the coincidence. Manhattan was an awfully large city to stumble into the one that got away while on the way to a job interview.

There was nothing left to do but stand and embrace, two soulmates reconnecting on a moving train. Strangers watched unabashedly drawn in by the significance of this reunion.

Were they attached to other people? Did they live anywhere near one another? Was this another chance meeting or was this where everything changed, and they finally got it right?

Nothing else mattered at that moment. They held each other and swayed with the movement of the train. All was aligned and right with the world again, simply because they were in the same place at the same time.

They have loved each other for longer than they realize. Feeling the absence of the past ten years was a drop in the bucket compared to the emptiness of knowing they once had the greatest love they would have in this lifetime.

The doors slid open. They were at her stop. A second chance at hello, a second chance for goodbye.

But not this time. He would never let her go a second time... that he knew of.

He took her hand, and they stepped out into the world together, as it was meant to be, in this lifetime.

"It's about damn time," he snips but smiles over to the other armchair at her. She smiles back comfortingly and asks the most important question: "But now what will we watch?"

Chapter 15

Good Love

Dear BFF, you wouldn't believe who I met last night! Walking toward me, under the streetlights…he'd just finished buttoning something into his shirt pocket and was getting ready to glance back up. Our eyes met; our footsteps slowed. The mutual recognition was as instantaneous as two particles.

Our grasp of its significance took a little longer.

Okay, here's what I saw, I don't know what he saw. He was taller than me, of course, and his hair was longer than mine is since my recent hack job.

He was extraordinarily good-looking, but I couldn't have said why, because his features aren't your everyday candy man.

His steps were long, purposeful, powerful, almost intimidating. His jaw had a dark hint of beard, and his upper lip had some mustache, not much, but more than I have, since I'm a girl. Yes, I noticed that he was a male, and I was a female.

However, and this is what's hard to explain, he looked like me. I mean he looked so much like me it took my breath away. How could this be? His body was totally different.

It was like seeing myself elongated, with facial hair, in a fun-house mirror. Nevertheless, here came me, walking down the street-lighted sidewalk toward me.

It was the expression in his eyes. I'm used to looking into my own eyes; I do it every time I put on my makeup. I never saw this expression in anyone else's eyes, and wouldn't expect to, because what I see in my eyes is no more nor less than 'me myself.' And what on earth was 'me myself' doing in someone else's eyes?

When I say I don't know what he saw, let me amend that: He saw my eyes. As I saw his.

Now, I've always been sure that there was only one of me in the universe. I wouldn't have even wanted another one. I had it all to myself. Mother, father, sibs, cousins, buddies, even you, you guys have been my company here on earth.

I've appreciated your presence, but I was never under some delusion that we were the same.

Often, too, I've looked into the eyes of another person and seen evidence of a humanity like mine. But, to see my very self? Think about it, wouldn't it scare you? Of course, it would. My breath stopped. My thinking stopped. I began to tremble.

His address was sharp, direct: "What the hell are you doing here?"

"What are you?" I countered.

We stopped walking and stood under one of the streetlights, panting, staring, trembling. He was the first to regain control.

He shoved his hands deep down into the pockets of his slacks. He wore slacks, something I would never wear because I'm a jeans and skirts type of gir and let out a shaky sigh. "Yeah, okay," he said. "I can see it,"

"What can you see?" I asked anxiously.

"That we're the same person."

"How could that be?"

"I know. But we are and you know it, too."

I glanced around, seeking escape. There was none. I was forced to admit we were the same person.

"Makes you kind of believe in parallel universes, huh?" His manner of questioning was impressively unnerving.

"I guess so. I'm not much into physics."

"Well, you are now."

I didn't see how this followed. But if we were the same person except in parallel universes, that didn't mean anything had to follow. We were the same person with different thoughts. That was obvious from the fact that he thought to wear slacks while I thought to eschew them.

There was a low concrete planter box outside a shop window, and we sat on it by silent consent. Neither of us could stand up. How did I know this? Because we were the same person. I know, I know, you're still not believing me.

"So," he said at last, "you were the girl."

"What girl?"

"The girl I wasn't."

"Yes, I was the girl and you were the boy my parents wished I'd been."

He laughed. I envied his laugh. He tossed his head back, and out came this bark, full of mystery. Was he laughing with me or at me?

But hey, if he was laughing at me, then wasn't he laughing at himself? Since we were the same? He said, "So, it was never really a choice, since here we both are. A lot of wasted angst, eh?"

"I don't see how you can be so light about it. I suffered a lot."

"Why?" He regarded me curiously. "You didn't have to."

"Of course, I had to. I was a girl. I wasn't going to be a captain, or a pilot, or any great thing. I was going to be short."

"I think you're cute short."

Don't think I didn't hear that blurt. But I went on, "Cute isn't what they wanted. They wanted dignity, reputation, that kind of thing.

Sure, I could have become a captain or a pilot, or a lawyer or even a judge, but I didn't want to, because I was a girl and my interests lay elsewhere."

"Elsewhere like where?"

"Dolls. I really cared about my dolls. Their wardrobe…their talking…their futures…"

"Huh. Yeah, okay." He scratched his head.

We were both wondering about each other, which is to say, wondering about ourselves. The night was getting cool.

I could feel the hairs prickling along my arms and I wondered, were his arm hairs prickling, too? And I wondered, to what degree were we bound together, anyway? I'd never been conscious of his presence before, so I wondered if I needed to be now.

He was looking at his shoe, way down there at the end of his outstretched leg, maybe still wondering why I'd cared about my dolls. I said, "I wonder why all of a sudden, we ran into each other.

Don't you have a life somewhere completely different, on a different plane?"

"I don't know about somewhere different," he said. "This is my street."

"It's mine, too."

"I've never seen you on it."

"But I've walked on it every day."

"Huh."

The moon came up. It was gibbous. Was it the same moon for him? I could ask him. It seemed strange to have to ask him anything, if we were the same person, but apparently, we didn't have all the same answers.

So, we were not entirely the same person. How far back did this go? At one time there was an egg and a bunch of sperm, and on that occasion, reality had split into two different universes, who knows why, whereupon he became him of that universe, and I became her of the other, if you see what I mean.

To think, here we'd be living alone, right on the same street, our every detail different, passing like ghosts and doubtless walking right through each other.

"Seeing myself as a man is more shocking than I thought it would be," I confessed. "Not that I've never tried to imagine it, but this is—this is—you know."

"Yes, I do know, actually."

"I never imagined I would be so—so—"

"So handsome? So tall?"

"Well, yes. I thought I'd look just like I do now except with a mustache and a penis."

"Interesting, because I haven't imagined myself as a woman, not seriously."

"I'm sure, because why would you?"

"Scientific curiosity if nothing else. But I must tell you, I've spent my whole life doing what's in front of me to do, and maybe that's a fundamental difference between us."

"Between men and women?"

"No. Between you and me."

"I do things," I protested. But in truth, as you know, dear BFF, I don't do a whole lot, because my nature is a quiet, waiting one, meditative and somewhat timid.

Then, was one of us realer than the other? I didn't know about him, but I can tell you I was very sure about the reality of my own existence, nor was I willing now to negotiate the matter.

"So," he said, as if reading my mind. "What are we going to do about this?"

"I'm not sure we need to do anything about it. We haven't exactly collided."

"Maybe you haven't. I have majorly collided."

I glanced at him, timidly. He was pretty shaken up. He'd started raking both hands through his hair as if his head were exploding from whatever was happening to him.

I wanted to put my arm around him and calm him, comfort him, but how to comfort someone whose entire foundation has been jerked out from under him? In fact, how to deal with my own explosion?

"Can we just go back to how things were?" I suggested.

"Can you??"

"Sure! Maybe…" I met his piercing glare. Nothing would do but truth. "No, I can't. Not anymore now that I've see you as everything I wanted to be. Tall. Strong. Masterful."

"And I suppose you're wishing I saw you as everything I wanted to be."

"Of course not! Nobody would want to be me. Would you…did you?"

"No."

"Because, obviously, you chose the more viable reality."

"Who says I chose? I was born the version I got, and I went with it. That was my strength."

"Ah. And I was born the version I got, and I didn't go with it, and that was my weakness."

"I didn't say that."

"But I am weak; I know I am. I mean, look at me."

He did look at me. I felt him doing it. Dear BFF, I wanted him to. I felt him looking, looking, looking, then away, then back, and with each look I felt weaker, until my weakness enveloped me like a warm, perfumed bath. Delicious, I can't describe how I loved him looking at me in all my weakness.

"You feel like you drew the wrong straw, then?" he persisted.

"Yes. Why couldn't I have been you?"

"Because there was already enough of me. There was none of you. What kind of a deal is that?"

"You are enough."

"No." He reached for my hand. "Not close."

"With you in the world, there was no need of me."

"There was." He took both my hands. "I needed someone to want."

"That's ridiculous…"

Ridiculous. I shut my mouth. If we were the same person, why were we arguing? He honestly didn't have a leg to stand on. He was everything; I was whatever was left over. I was a short straw.

I wasn't captain, pilot, lawyer, or judge. I wasn't presently even on a salary, having no job, and of course my dolls I'd loved so much were long gone, so what could I bring to the table? My very hair was scant compared to his.

I couldn't grow a beard, and I didn't need to see him jump to know he could jump way higher than I could. I stood up, smoothing my skirt down over my rump, saying, "Anyway, I think it would be impossible for two people who are actually the same person to have a meaningful conversation."

"We've been having one," he pointed out, standing as well.

"See? You are even reasonable." I frowned up into his face. "And tall."

"Right," he said. "And you are unreasonable and short."

"Yes. If we were Siamese twins, we would have to kill each other."

He barked that laugh…

But then he started looking around, over my head and down the street. I'd forgotten he had been on his way to somewhere else; evidently, he remembered.

Oh no, he was going to leave. At any rate, I supposed his leaving would answer the question of what we do now. I hugged my shoulders and wished I'd brought a jacket.

"Well, then," he put out a hand. "It was good to meet you, self. I sincerely hope your universe gives you whatever you ask from it."

"And I, too," I said. I didn't want to shake hands. I had this dreadful realization that my universe wasn't going to give me whatever I asked of it, because I hadn't asked it. And so…and so…

"Wait," I said, catching his arm. "Is it possible for people from different universes to fall in love?"

His raised eyebrow made me regret my question. "I wouldn't count on it," he said.

"Why not?"

"Because you already have."

"What??"

"You fell in love with yourself when you were born and then you let other people talk you out of it, on the grounds of your being weak and short and not a pilot. What kind of love is that?"

"But if it's true?"

"Who cares if they think it's true? Look, love's hard enough for people who share the same universe. But for people like us." He dropped his gaze to my shoulders. "You're freezing."

"For people like us?" I prompted.

"It must be good love. That's the only way to bridge the gap." He wasn't leaving.

I could have asked him then what he meant by something as vague as 'good love,' but as you can imagine, I didn't want to, in case the answer would be something I didn't want to hear.

In case he was warning me I had to start with loving myself before I moved on to loving him otherwise there'd be no use my asking the universe for anything.

Okay, well, yes, I knew that was what he meant.

I knew because I am not stupid; I just act like it. I'm not even short. I'm not lacking in any way that would negatively quantify 'good love.'

Good God, I am the very quintessence of captain, pilot, lawyer, judge, or tall person! I'm a person who knows how to love, 'good love' and that, right there, is my worthiness. Therefore, yes, I can ask the universe for what I really, truly desire.

And I did ask. Bravely, strongly, I did ask. His universe or mine, I'll never know for sure; both understood my heart.

So, dear BFF, I wanted you to be the first to hear the news. Because parallel lines can't meet, but they can get awfully, awfully close and they can go on traveling that way, side by side, far beyond the edge of the visible universe.

Chapter 16

Last Wish

They were coming. Sophie could sense it. Her hand, gripped tightly around Leo's hand, squeezed even more. Faster, she wanted to say to him, we must get out of here! But if she even breathed a word, Leo would be done for.

She could already envision him in her head, ripped to shreds by the wolves with his bones picked clean. Afterall, she had seen this many times before, though she tried not to think about it and focus on running.

Their run sped up to a sprint, with Leo immediately understanding her signal. Ahead of them, the path split in two.

One led deeper into the forest, while the other led out, back to the city of Gilder. It took all of Sophie's willpower to ignore the path that led out and follow the one that plunged farther into the forest darkness.

If they faced the wolves, the wolves would kill them quickly and swiftly without hesitation. Pain would be minimal. But if they faced the city of Gilder, the humans, Sophie could only begin to imagine what they would do to Leo. Of course, she and Leo had once been citizens of Gilder as well, but those humans were different.

Overcome with greed, they had no morals left–practically as kind as a bloodthirsty monster. For Sophie, it was easy to escape a living hell like that. She always kept a pocketknife in her sleeve, which she would use to slit her neck whenever she became cornered.

The world would rewind, back to the time before she and Leo ran away. For someone as old as Sophie, time had lost its meaning. She had lost track of how many lives she had been through.

In fact, all her memories were foggy, and she couldn't really remember anything about her first life. The only thing that came up when she racked her brain for memories was a pretty woman with black hair, and a child around her age.

Sophie shook her head, focusing on the chase. If she wanted to get out of there alive, she couldn't dwell on past lives.

The smell of the wolves became fainter as they ran. Leo's pace slowed down as he began to tire, and, noticing this, Sophie adjusted hers and they slowed to a walking speed.

Above the treetops, a soft orange glow began to spread. The first birds started to chirp, and soon the eerie darkness of the ominous night sky was erased as the forest became alive with cheerful sounds and brightening surroundings.

Looking around, Sophie noticed a crack between two great boulders. The crack, just big enough for an adolescent to squeeze through, was the entrance to a bigger cave.

Not bigger much, though, Sophie noted as she peered through the crack. The space inside was only enough for two people to curl up uncomfortably. Still, it was better than having to sleep in a tree, so she and Leo pushed their way in one after the other.

Since the crack was so small, dangerous predators like the wolves wouldn't be able to get in, so Sophie decided that a watch wasn't needed today. After whispering this to Leo, they curled up against each other and drifted off to sleep.

A woman, deathly pale, lay on a bed. Next to her bed, a young girl played with the woman's hair.

The girl, a younger Sophie, stopped her playing to look at the woman. In sleep, she looked so peaceful, like a painting frozen in time. Her pale face was tinged with the slightest bit of blush powder.

Her moving chest, the only sign of life, rose and fell, as if getting weaker each time. Long, black lashes marked her eyes, which fluttered open as Sophie stared.

"My child…come," she beckoned, some of her black hair falling off the bed as she turned.

"Mother, why are you in bed? Father won't tell me, and Brother says you are dying. You must get up and tell him he is wrong!"

"I'm afraid…Reynold is right."

"That's not true! You promised you would live to see me become an adult."

"I'm sorry, Sophie. Life is a fleeting thing"

She broke into a fit of coughing. A metal arm extended from the wall holding a cup of water and slowly poured the liquid down the woman's throat. Sophie watched silently as the coughing stopped.

"Well, it looks like it's time for me to go."

"Are you finally going to prove Brother wrong?"

The stubborn woman shook her head. "I am to meet my parents."

"Silly Mother! Don't you know Grandma and Grandpa have already passed on? Stay with me."

"I-I can't."

"What do you mean?"

"I won't be able to see you become an adult… Maybe in another life…"

Her voice became quieter as her eyes closed for the last time.

Sophie woke up with a start. Her mother had died in front of her. And her last words, were they an indication of what was to come?

This wasn't the first time Sophie had dreamed of her past, but they had never been so clear and complete. Plus, this dream revealed her mother's death, which hadn't been shown in previous dreams. Her mother was one of the only people she could remember from past lives the other being a child who looked around her age. Which, come to think of it, Sophie couldn't ever seem to remember much about.

Wavy brown hair fell to their shoulders, a fierce flame in their golden eyes- Leo's golden eyes. Sophie looked down, and there was Leo, eyes shut and still asleep. A ray of light came through the crack, hitting his light brown hair, and making it look orange, red even, like fire.

Leo was stunning. Too feminine to call handsome, he had fair skin and soft features. His brown hair looked like fire when light hit it. Like the rest of his clan, Leo had glimmering yellow eyes, believed to have real gold in them.

In fact, legends say that they can foretell, or in other words omniscient eyes. Those eyes were valuable. Precious to the point that Leo's clan was exterminated solely because the other Gilder people desired their rare eyes.

Hundreds of eye-less bodies found a home in the blood-soaked soil of Gilder that night. The only reason Leo wasn't one of them was because Sophie had saved him. She freed him from the sure death that awaited him. She pulled him out of the prison, and into the dark forest.

To say that she did it only because she had nothing to lose would be wrong. Even if she could die and stay dead, Sophie would still choose to help Leo. In fact, she wanted to die completely, as it would be the only way to escape the loop.

Every time they got close to the end of the forest, it was always either the wolves or bounty hunters that killed them. Although she and Leo were now both seventeen, Sophie would probably be around a hundred years old if all her lives were added together. And yet, time and time again, Sophie chose to help Leo escape, for he was her happiness.

In the spring after her mother's death, her brother Reynold followed. Her father would never be the same again.

When the massacre of Leo's clan happened, she had helped him on a whim without success, only to find that time would rewind to the darkest point of her life, right after her mother and brother's death.

With the seemingly infinite loop of misery, Leo had been her only light. She didn't remember when she had met him, but his golden eyes seemed to guide her back towards happiness.

Then when the massacre happened, she decided to help him. If life was meaningless either way, Sophie wanted to at least help Leo achieve a happy life, since it was impossible for her.

She had heard of cities on the other side of the forest from her mother. This was a memory that had stayed. Those cities were friendlier, and they would be able to give Leo the ideal life.

Sophie called those cities, the Better Cities. A childish name, for sure, but an accurate description.

As Sophie stared at Leo, she was shocked to see the resemblance between him and the kid from her dreams. She couldn't help but wonder if the child was from Leo's clan, or if that was him from a long time ago.

Leo's eyes suddenly opened, contacting the light. For a moment, he looked like a sculpture of gold, before reality set in and Leo flinched at the brightness.

"Is it sunset already?" he asked Sophie, drowsily rubbing his eyes.

Sophie peeked through the crack, only to see that the sun was still high in the sky. Their bodies hadn't yet adjusted to the new nocturnal schedule, which was why they couldn't sleep peacefully through the day.

"No, you can rest more. I'll go out to see if there are any berries we can eat."

As Sophie began to squeeze through the hole, Leo called to her.

"When we get to the Better Cities, what do you want to do?"

"What do you mean?"

"Like a job. I was thinking I could be a pharmacist!"

"That's silly. The robots have already taken over that field, though you could still be a doctor."

"Oh. Well, you'll be an adult soon, so what do you want to do?"

Ignoring him, Sophie crawled out of the cave. Truth be told, in her many lives, never had she become an adult. Death was always so easy to receive.

Though, at the time, she was seventeen and her birthday was in two days, meaning that she would have to find a job as soon as they got to the

Better Cities. Whether or not they could even get there was uncertain, though.

The sun was beginning to set when Sophie came back. She and Leo quickly ate the berries she had found, before saying goodbye to the small cave and setting out again.

The North Star served as an eternal guide. Sophie was grateful for that, otherwise she would long be lost in the seemingly endless trees.

The wolves appeared every other day, so their trek that day was safe and without trouble, except a few other nocturnal critters scrambling about.

Day passed with one person sleeping while the other collected food and kept watch, the roles switching a few times.

The only notable event was another one of Sophie's dreams, in which the golden-eyed kid appeared. After seeing him up close, Sophie determined him to be a boy, who seemed more and more like Leo the more they interacted.

In the dream, they were in a field of grass, talking like friends, and though Sophie couldn't remember the content of their conversation, it was a refreshing break from reality. At the end, when Sophie asked the boy for his name, he only smiled and said,

"You already know."

Night would be dangerous that day. The wolves were back, hungrier than ever for the humans that had escaped their grasp last time.

Sophie and Leo were extremely close to the Better Cities, and if they survived that night, their goal would finally be achieved.

The first half of the night was safe, but as the timer for dawn began to tick, the wolves' scent became stronger.

The first wolf appeared without warning. Sophie hadn't sensed anything until it appeared. She and Leo had maintained a brisk walk when Leo suddenly whispered a question.

"Isn't today your birthday?"

"What're you talking about? Hush!" Sophie had whispered back fiercely. Leo was right of course-midnight had just passed, and it was a new day, but even a whisper could bring death.

"You're finally an adult! Your mother would be happy," Leo continued, ignoring Sophie's warning.

Hearing this, Sophie's interest was piqued. "How would you know?"

"My clan's eyes are all-knowing. Why would you not remember? Is it that you can't remember?"

"O-of course I remember."

"Be happy, Sophie! You broke the loop!" he chirped excitedly, suddenly stopping in his tracks.

"What are you doing? Keep running!"

"You don't understand, Sophie. Your life won't ever repeat again! You're free!"

Leo's voice was cut off as the wolf appeared. Suddenly, his mysterious comment didn't matter anymore, and Sophie grabbed his hand.

They ran as fast as they could, not paying attention to the North Star anymore. But whether by chance, or by fate, the houses of the Better Cities came into view as they ran.

All of that was irrelevant, though, and when wolf after wolf appeared, it seemed that they would die again.

Through all this, Leo surprisingly remained calm and even chatted a bit.

"Oh, are those the Better Cities?"

"Wow, they look advanced!"

"Say, shouldn't you celebrate? You're an adult now!"

"Shut up!" Sophie snapped. "The wolves are here! Can't you see? Just run!"

As the first few houses appeared, Sophie began to scream and yell for help. Perhaps because it was night, most people were asleep, and her first cries for help went unanswered.

The wolves were gaining on them. One of them even managed to rip off a bit of Sophie's sweater, causing blood to trickle out. The smell of iron only made the wolves crazier, and it didn't help that Sophie tripped on a branch.

Her ankle made a dreadful snapping sound, and Sophie collapsed on the ground.

Leo stopped to help her up, but she shoved him away. By that time a few people had heard the commotion and came out with flashlights, trying to shoo the wolves away. Still, they were too far away, and with her ankle twisted, Sophie couldn't run anymore.

"Run, Leo! Don't worry about me! I'll be reborn again, but YOU must survive!" Sophie screamed at Leo, shoved him, and hit him, yet Leo didn't budge.

"Not this time," he murmured.

"What?"

"Your mother's wish. It's been fulfilled. You're an adult now, remember?"

"What does that have to do w–"

"Get away, you, guys!" a person shouted at them. It was a middle-aged man, one of the people helping to drive the wolves away.

In his hand he held a gun, which was aimed at the wolf closest to them. "I may shoot you guys by accident if you don't get away right now!" he yelled at them.

Leo continued, as if the man's words were nothing more than wind to his ears. "Your mother wished for you to grow up. And yet, in all your lives, you've never become one–up until now."

"So does that mean the loop has broken?"

"Yes."

Upon hearing this, Sophie only pushed harder. "Go away, Leo! You still have a bright future! You're finally in the Better Cities, why aren't you moving?!" Sophie's voice rose into a shriek towards the end.

"Would you believe me if I said I wanted to be with you?"

"No! The wolf is close, run away while you still can!" Sophie pleaded, turning her gaze to the approaching canine.

"Sophie, look at me."

"I'M TIRED, OKAY?!" Sophie cried, pausing for a moment. "Sorry, it's just, I'm tired. Tired of life, death, everything.

So right now, you're telling me that I can finally rest, forever, without waking up again, and I want to die!"

Tears spilled from her eyes as Sophie vented her pent-up despair, all the years she spent longing to go to the place her mother and brother were, all her loneliness and sadness, all put together as she released her emotions.

"I tried repeatedly to protect you, to get you to the Better Cities, and here we are! But we'll never be together, Leo. I can't drag you down with me."

"Guys, I'm shooting...if you want to live then get out of the way!" called the man with the gun as he pulled the trigger, sending the bullets towards them and the wolf next to them.

Time seemed to slow down. The bullets, the wolf, and everything else around them seemed to go in slow motion. It was as if the yells and shouts around them all faded to white noise, and Sophie could only see Leo, and vice versa.

Like they were in their own world. In one sudden movement, Leo embraced Sophie, breathing into her ear as he did so.

"I just want to be with you...let's rest together."

Unexpectedly, death wasn't painful. The bullet pierced their bodies and warm blood splattered across the ground, but to Sophie and Leo, death welcomed them gently. Like the benevolent rain after a drought.

It brought a sort of peace and tranquility, which they were grateful for. As the heat of their bodies faded, their souls seemed to drift away as well. To a faraway place, where all their loved ones were. Where there was no pain, no anguish, and no sorrow...just death.

Chapter 17

Not Meant to Be

"From the moment I met you, I knew there was something special about you," he starts, tucking a loose strand of my curly brown hair behind my ear.

I smile, thinking of the first time I heard that line. The boy who said it was my first love. For a time, I thought, the one. But he's not the one standing in front of me now. Instead, it's Adrian, my boyfriend of four years, wearing that cheeky little grin of his.

"You have this warmth and kindness that shines through in everyone you meet, and everything you do. You make me laugh, you challenge me, and you undoubtedly make me a better person," Adrian continues, and I think to myself, I made him a better person too.

I gave him everything I could at that age. I wanted nothing more than to be a pair of reckless teenagers in love, but my parents didn't approve of me dating outside my culture. But, at that time, nothing could keep me away from the rush of adrenaline I felt with you. Nothing, and no one.

I look out to the ocean and watch the tide roll in and out as Adrian recounts the story of how we met. His mother approached mine at a wedding to ask for my number because he was so nervous, he knocked his drink all over his suit before he could leave his table. But you never hesitated to approach me first, Vic.

I remember sitting at the lumpy red booth in the back of Enzo's Pizzeria after class, loading my plain slice up with an absurd number of toppings when you came over and introduced yourself to me.

You pushed your baseball hat backwards before you extended your hand, to give me a better view of your face. But I didn't hear a word that came out of your mouth, and you knew it. I was mesmerized by your amber eyes, wondering what school you went to, how often you worked out, and if you had a girlfriend or not.

You laughed as I spaced out while holding your hand, and it sounded like something you didn't do very often. You then pointed to my tray, asking to borrow the parmesan cheese for your friend so he could do the exact same thing.

I looked down at my train wreck of a pizza slice and I practically turned as red as the sauce on it. You thought I was being cute and came back later to give me napkins. The bottom one in the pile had your name and number written on it.

Adrian grabs my hand and rubs his thumb across the back of it. He's moved on to our first kiss story, his blue eyes mirroring the evening sky when he talks. He was so proud of himself that night, saving up for a week to take me to the fanciest steakhouse in town for our first official date.

After dinner, I kissed him on my building's front steps, because I didn't have to worry about the doorman telling my parents. I always had you drop me off three blocks away, just to play it safe.

Our first kiss was something out of a movie. It was a rainy summer day, and I was lifeguarding. You biked to me in the pouring rain just to stand at the gate in sopping wet clothes, to tell me you loved me. I, again, was embarrassed because the heat always flushed to my cheeks around you.

I remember looking around to make sure no one was around to watch me jump into your arms. No matter what, I had to live with the fear of my parents finding out.

My mind was screaming what if they find out, what if they disown me, what if they hate me, and yet I pressed my lips to yours like you were this obscene craving I had to get a fix of.

I slowly drop Adrian's hand and cross my arms, resting the palms of my hands on my shoulders, to hug myself to find that same warmth I felt back then. With you, I felt safe. With Adrian, I find solace.

The hem of my sundress picks up with the sea breeze as my eyes greet my boyfriend the same way one sees their reflection: loving it in pieces but cringing at it. I love his floppy brunette hair, movie star smile, and his uncanny ability to make me laugh.

I jump at the fact that he's everything my parents expected from me, and I hate the fact that you weren't enough for them. For me.

"Ness, I want to…" Adrian clears his throat and carefully rubs the palms of his hands across his black slacks.

"Want to what?" I interrupt, the mere mention of my nickname sending me into overdrive. You were the one to give me that nickname, and I can't believe it stuck by me all these years. Even after you were out of my life for good.

Before I can submit to the next wave of nostalgia coursing through my brain, I realize Adrian is on one knee, and he's not tying his shoelaces.

A little black box peeks out at me through his left side pocket. My throat starts to hitch, and my pulse becomes a slave to my anxiety. How didn't I see that when we were walking in the sand?

I was lying on your chest when I confided I never thought I'd get married, in any traditional sense, at least.

That I believed I was never meant to throw a lavish wedding, because I knew my family would not come if my parents refused to accept my spouse.

That I knew whatever love I was given, no matter how special, I would elope if they weren't what my parents wanted. That I didn't want kids if they wouldn't be cherished by their grandparents.

I remember sobbing into the soft cotton fabric of your hoodie, the one I'd always end up stealing because no matter how much it was washed, it still carried the scent of your ridiculously strong cologne.

Your heartbeat probably as fast as mine is right at this very moment, except it was out of anger more than anxiety.

You tried to kiss me and comfort me and tell me I'm strong enough to survive life without the acceptance of my parents. But no matter how many times you told me, I never believed you.

Because I was scared, we wouldn't work. You'd eventually get tired of sneaking around and grow to resent me for it, and I'd let my anxiety eat me whole, until there was no one left to hate but myself for treating our relationship like a dirty little secret.

My fingertips are digging into the flesh of my shoulders as I fight the tears brimming in my eyes. The smile I have plastered on my face must be working because Adrian is getting quite worked up himself.

I see his hands are shaky as they open the little black box, as if its contents are more precious to him than life itself. They're happy tears, Ness. You're happy now. You love this man, he's so good to you.

"I promise to be there for you: as a best friend, a partner, and a soulmate, through thick and thin. To support you and encourage you, and to love you with all my heart," Adrian says, his eyes getting as equally glassy as mine.

I wanted it to be you, Vic. But we kissed like we were starving, hugged like we were protecting each other from the outside world, and made love as if our lives depended on it, as if we knew we'd have limited time together.

You loved me fiercely because you saw a future, I did it because I knew what we had was fleeting. I'm just not as strong as you think I am.

Remember our fights, how I'd say the most vicious words to you to get you to hate me? I needed you to hate me. That was the only way I could move on.

"Vanessa, will you marry me?" Adrian says as he lifts the ring to meet my eyeline.

The tears fall from my eyes and flood my vision, my only lifeline being the glare from the setting sun off that gorgeous diamond ring.

You definitely would've found his ring choice basic, because you told me I deserved more than just a diamond. You said you'd want an emerald set in the center with a halo of little diamonds for me, to match one of your favorite things about me: my green eyes.

Maybe, if I'd stood up to my parents then, I'd be here on this beach with you today. Maybe, in another life, I'd have your ring on my finger. But, in this one, I craved my parent's acceptance more than I craved to be loved by you.

Wiping the tears from my eyes, I cave to the one word that will make you nothing but a distant memory.

"Yes," I say to Adrian, with the best and brightest smile I can ever give. "Of course, I will marry you."

He flashes that same Hollywood smile I love right back at me, sliding the ring you'd hate on my finger. Once he's back on his two feet, I grab his face and pull his mouth to mine.

Because that's the way I know I'd kiss you, in another life.

Chapter 18

Love That Kills Never Dies

The night was expanding its wings over the city with its velvety darkness. The kind that slows down a man's heart rhythm, slowly puts her hands around a man's neck, and holds on to him until night is over.

The night was a sweet, warm black that hugged him no matter what, and within its safety he could finally breathe.

His heart was heavy with the weight of love, and as she kissed his neck and whispered his name, every fiber of his being was consumed by the intensity of the moment.

He longed for it to last, but the night was merciless, and time slipped away too quickly. Such a shame the whisper wasn't long enough, the cuddle not tight enough.

Such a shame the night was too dark and swallowed every chance of someone's star brightening it up.

As he lay there, memories of her flooded his mind, filling him with a longing so deep that it seemed to seep into his very soul.

The gentle touch of her skin, the warmth of her embrace, and the way she called out his name echoed through his mind like a haunting melody.

In her arms, he had found a sanctuary, a place where all his worries and fears could be cast aside.

Although she was gone and the coldness of the night seeped into his bones, as if his heart were a wide-open door to the frigid wind, slamming shut just to reopen.

He felt his drowning eyes and simply chose to listen to her whisper instead. He did not whisper back.

But now, as this night grew longer, he found himself alone once more, the emptiness of his bed a constant reminder of what he had lost. His heart ached with a deep sense of longing, as if a part of him had been torn away.

He held onto her pillow, searching for any trace of her scent, but it had already begun to fade, carried away by the cruel winds of the night.

Yet still, he clung to the hope that one day they would be together again, that the night would once more wrap them in its warm embrace.

For she was his ecstasy, his natural drug. The night may be dark and endless, but if he had her, he knew that he could find his way through it.

As he felt the nausea rise within him, he hastily grabbed his coat and left the room. The sudden rush of cool air hit him as he opened the door, and an unfamiliar light flooded the once-dark room.

As he walked into the darkness of the night, the street seemed to take on a new life of its own. The streetlights flickered on and off, casting an eerie glow on the otherwise pitch-black surroundings.

The empty street seemed to stretch out for miles in front of him, with shadows creeping up from the sides like silent observers.

The contrast between the dimly lit street and the enveloping darkness gave him ghost-like features, as if he was a specter wandering through a world of the living.

The sound of his footsteps echoed through the empty street, creating an unsettling rhythm that seemed to punctuate the stillness of the night. His coat rustled in the wind, flapping like wings on his back as he walked through the abandoned street.

The buildings around him loomed high, casting deep shadows that seemed to swallow up any light that dared to stray too close.

Despite the uneasy feeling in the pit of his stomach, he couldn't help but feel a sense of awe at the stark beauty of the night.

The way the streetlights illuminated the darkness, and the way the shadows danced across the pavement, gave the world an otherworldly feel that was both unsettling and captivating at the same time. Yet again, his thoughts were drawn to her absence.

Once, he ran through fire for her, his love burning bright as the flames that licked at his feet. But now, all that remained was the ashen memory of what they once had.

The wind carried the debris of their love away, scattering it like a macabre confetto. Each heartbeat, more of it flew away, and he could only watch in silent agony as the cinders of their once beautiful love scattered into nothingness.

His tears were proof that their love was gone, destroyed by the fire of their own passions.

The night had grown even darker, the streetlights flickering out one by one until he was left standing in complete darkness. He couldn't see anything, couldn't hear anything, and for a moment, he thought he had died and gone to hell.

But then he felt a cold hand on his shoulder, and he knew that he was not alone. He turned around, but there was no one there. Only the darkness, the cold, and the feeling of dread that seemed to be suffocating him.

He tried to run, but his legs wouldn't move. He was trapped, a prisoner of the night, and there was no escape. The night seemed to be mocking him, reminding him of all that he had lost. He tried to shake off the feeling of hopelessness, but it clung to him like a heavy shroud, suffocating him with its weight.

He stopped yet again at the end of the street, staring out at the vast emptiness that lay ahead of him. There was no direction, no destination, no purpose. He was lost, adrift in a sea of darkness without her compass to guide him.

It was as if the universe had conspired against him, leaving him stranded in a desolate world with nothing but his shattered dreams, while she was far away passing time in someone else's arms.

But in the depths of his despair, he found himself almost instinctively walking towards the bench where they had first met, memories of their time together came rushing back.

He remembered how they used to sit here for hours, talking, and laughing as if nothing else in the world mattered. But now, the bench seemed to be a desolate place, a graveyard of their love that had died not long ago.

The paint on the bench was peeling, and the wood was rotting away, a reflection of the decay that had taken hold of their lives. The once vibrant colors had faded into a dull, lifeless shade, much like the spark that had once existed between them.

He sat down on the bench, feeling the cold metal dig into his skin. He closed his eyes and breathed in the scent of the decaying wood, feeling as though he had been transported back to a time when they were still together.

But the nostalgia was fleeting, and he was soon reminded of the reality of their situation. They had parted ways on bad terms, their love turned bitter and sour like a poison that had seeped into their veins.

As he sat there, the darkness of the night seemed to encroach upon him, engulfing him in a blanket of shadows.

The silence of the night was deafening, broken only by the sound of his own ragged breaths. The bench was now a symbol of their broken love, a reminder of the pain and heartache that seemed to have consumed him more than it had her.

He knew that he could not go back to the way things were, that their love was forever lost in the darkness of the night. As he got up from the bench, he felt a sense of finality wash over him, as if he had finally accepted the reality of their situation.

He walked away from the bench, leaving behind the remnants of their love to decay and crumble away.

The night was dark, but he knew that he had to keep moving forward, back to square one, in the hopes of finding a new love that might fade or wither away on a cold night such as this one but never truly die.

Chapter 19

The Origin of Short Stories

A short story, also known as a nouvelle, is a piece of prose fiction that can typically be read in a single sitting and focuses on a self-contained incident or series of linked incidents, with the intent of evoking a single effect or mood.

The short story is one of the oldest types of literature and has existed in the form of legends, mythic tales, folk tales, fairy tales, tall tales, fables, and anecdotes in various ancient communities around the world. The modern short story developed in the early 19th century.

The Meaning of a Short Story

The short story is a crafted form. Short stories make use of plot, resonance, and other dynamic components as in a novel, but typically to a lesser degree.

While the short story is largely distinct from the novel or novella/short novel, authors generally draw from a common pool of literary techniques.[citation needed] The short story is sometimes referred to as a genre.

Determining what exactly defines a short story has been recurrently problematic. A classic definition of a short story is that one should be able to read it in one sitting, a point most notably made in Edgar Allan Poe's essay "The Philosophy of Composition" 1846.

H.G. Wells described the purpose of the short story as "The jolly art, of making something very bright and moving; it may be horrible or pathetic or funny or profoundly illuminating, having only this essential, that it should take from fifteen to fifty minutes to read aloud."

According to William Faulkner, a short story is character-driven, and a writer's job is to "…trot along behind him with a paper and pencil trying to keep up long enough to put down what he says and does."

Some authors have argued that a short story must have a strict form. Somerset Maugham thought that the short story "must have a definite design, which includes a point of departure, a climax and a point of test; in other words, it must have a plot".

Hugh Walpole had a similar view: "A story should be a story; a record of things happening full of incidents, swift movements, unexpected development, leading through suspense to a climax and a satisfying denouement."

This view of the short story as a finished product of art is however opposed by Anton Chekov, who thought that a story should have neither a beginning nor an end. It should just be a "slice of life", presented suggestively. In his stories, Chekov does not round off the end but leaves it to the readers to draw their own conclusions.

Sukumar Azhikode defined a short story as "a brief prose narrative with an intense episodic or anecdotal effect".

Flannery O'Connor emphasized the need to consider what exactly is meant by the descriptor short.

Short story writers may define their works as part of the artistic and personal expression of the form. They may also attempt to resist categorization by genre and fixed formation.

William Boyd, a British author, and short story writer, has said the following:

A short story seems to answer something very deep in our nature as if, for the duration of its telling, something special has been created, some essence of our experience extrapolated, some temporary sense has been made of our common, turbulent journey towards the grave and oblivion.

In the 1880s, the term "short story" acquired its modern meaning – having initially referred to children's tales.

During the early to mid-20th century, the short story underwent expansive experimentation which further hindered attempts to comprehensively provide a definition.

Longer stories that cannot be called novels are sometimes considered "novellas" or novelettes and, like short stories, may be collected into the more marketable form of "collections", of stories previously unpublished or published, but elsewhere.

Sometimes, authors who do not have the time or money to write a novella or novel decide to write short stories instead, working out a deal with a popular website or magazine to publish them for profit.

Around the world, the modern short story is comparable to lyrics, dramas, novels, and essays, although examination of it as a major literary form remains diminished.

In terms of length, the word count is typically anywhere from 1,000 to 4,000 for short stories; however, some have 15,000 words and are still classed as short stories.

Stories of fewer than 1,000 words are sometimes referred to as "short stories", or "flash fiction".

Short stories have no set length. In terms of word count, there is no official demarcation between an anecdote, a short story, and a novel.

Rather, the form's parameters are given by the rhetorical and practical context in which a given story is produced and considered so that what constitutes a short story may differ between genres, countries, eras, and commentators.

Like the novel, the short story's predominant shape reflects the demands of the available markets for publication, and the evolution of the form seems closely tied to the evolution of the publishing industry and the submission guidelines of its constituent houses.

As a point of reference for the genre writer, the Science Fiction and Fantasy Writers of America define short story length in the Nebula Awards for science fiction submission guidelines as having fewer than 7,500 words.

Short stories date back to oral storytelling traditions which originally produced epics such as the Ramayana, the Mahabharata, and Homer's Iliad and Odyssey.

Oral narratives were often told in the form of rhyming or rhythmic verse, often including recurring sections or, in the case of Homer, Homeric epithets.

Such stylistic devices often acted as mnemonics for easier recall, rendition, and adaptation of the story. Short sections of verse might focus on individual narratives that could be told at one sitting.

The overall arc of the tale would emerge only through the telling of multiple such sections.

According to Azhikode, the short story has existed "in the most ancient times as the parable, the adventure-story of men, gods and demons, the account of daily events, the joke".

All languages have had variations of short tales and stories almost since their inception.

Emerging in the 17th century from oral storytelling traditions, the short story has grown to encompass a body of work so diverse as to defy easy characterization. "The short story as a carefully contrived literary form is of modern origin", wrote Azhikode.

Chapter 20

Early Examples of short stories

1790–1850

Early examples of short stories were published separately between 1790 and 1810, but the first true collections of short stories appeared between 1810 and 1830 in several countries.

The first short stories in the United Kingdom were gothic tales like Richard Cumberland's "remarkable narrative", "The Poisoner of Montremos" (1791).

Novelists such as Sir Walter Scott and Charles Dickens also wrote influential short stories during this time. Germany soon followed the United Kingdom's example by producing short stories; the first collection of short stories was by Heinrich von Kleist in 1810 and 1811.

Edgar Allan Poe became one of the first American short story writers, taking a cosmopolitan approach to writing. His concise technique, deemed the "single effect", has had tremendous influence on the formation of the modern short story.

1850–1900

In the latter half of the 19th century, the growth of print magazines and journals created a strong demand for short fiction of between 3,000 and 15,000 words. In 1890s Britain, literary periodicals such as The

Yellow Book, Black & White, and The Strand Magazine popularized the short story.

Britain was not alone in the endeavor to strengthen the short story movement. French author Guy de Maupassant composed the short stories "Boule de Suif" ("Ball of Fat", 1880) and "L'Inutile Beauté" ("The Useless Beauty", 1890), which are important examples of French realism. Russian author Anton Chekhov was also influential in the movement.

In the late nineteenth and early twentieth century in India, many writers created short stories centered on daily life and the social scene of the different socioeconomic groups.

Rabindranath Tagore published more than 150 short stories on the lives of the poor and oppressed such as peasants, women, and villagers under colonial misrule and exploitation. Sarat Chandra Chattopadhyay, Tagore's contemporary, was another pioneer in Bengali short stories.

Chattopadhyay's stories focused on the social scenario of rural Bengal and the lives of common people, especially the oppressed classes. The prolific Indian author of short stories Munshi Premchand, pioneered the genre in the Hindustani language, writing over 200 short stories and many novels in a style characterized by realism and an unsentimental and authentic introspection into the complexities of Indian society.

In the United States, Washington Irving was responsible for creating some of the first short stories of American origin, "The Legend of Sleepy Hollow" and "Rip Van Winkle".

Twenty years later, in 1884, Brander Matthews, the first American professor of dramatic literature, published The Philosophy of the Short-Story. During that same year, Matthews was the first one to name the emerging genre "short story". Another theorist of narrative fiction was Henry James, who produced some of the most influential short narratives of the time.

The spread of the short story movement continued into South America, specifically Brazil. The novelist Machado de Assis was an important short story writer from Brazil at the time, under the influences of Xavier de Maistre, Laurence Sterne, Guy de Maupassant, among others.[citation needed] At the end of the 19th century, the writer João do Rio became popular by short stories about the bohemianism. Lima Barreto wrote about the former slaves and nationalism in Brazil, with his most recognized work being Triste Fim de Policarpo Quaresma.

1900–1945

In the United Kingdom, periodicals like The Strand Magazine and Story-Teller contributed to the popularity of the short story.[citation needed] Several authors during this time wrote short stories centered on the devices of satire and humor.

One such author, Hector Hugh Munro (1870–1916), also known by his pen name of Saki, wrote satirical short stories about Edwardian England. P.G. Wodehouse published his first collection of comical stories about the valet, Jeeves, in 1917. Other common genres of short stories during the early to mid 1900s in England were detective stories and thrillers.

Many of these detective stories were written by authors such as G.K. Chesterton, Agatha Christie, and Dorothy L. Sayers. Graham Greene wrote his collection of short stories, Twenty-One Stories, between 1929 and 1954.

Many of these short stories are classified in the genres of thriller, suspense, or even horror. The European short story movement during this time was not unique to England.

In Ireland, James Joyce published his short story collection Dubliners in 1914. These stories, written in a more accessible style than his later novels, are based on careful observation of the inhabitants of his birth city.

In the first half of the 20th century, several high-profile American magazines such as The Atlantic Monthly, Harper's Magazine, The New Yorker, Scribner's, The Saturday Evening Post, Esquire, and The Bookman published short stories in each issue.

The demand for quality short stories was so great and the money paid so well that F. Scott Fitzgerald repeatedly turned to short-story writing to pay his numerous debts. His first collection, Flappers and Philosophers, appeared in book form in 1920.

Ernest Hemingway's concise writing style was perfectly suited for shorter fiction. Influenced by the short stories of Stephen Crane and Jack London, Hemingway's work "marks a new phase in the history of the short story".

The creation and study of the short story as a medium began to emerge as an academic discipline due to Blanche Colton Williams' "groundbreaking work on structure and analysis of the short story"]:128 and her publication of A Handbook on Short Story Writing (1917), described as "the first practical aid to growing young writers that was put on the market in this country."

In Uruguay, Horacio Quiroga became one of the most influential short story writers in the Spanish language.

With a clear influence from Edgar Allan Poe, he had a great skill in using the supernatural and the bizarre to show the struggle of man and animal to survive. He also excelled in portraying mental illness and hallucinatory states.

In India, Saadat Hasan Manto, the master of the short story in the Urdu language, is revered for his exceptional depth, irony, and sardonic humor.

The author of some 250 short stories, radio plays, essays, reminiscences, and a novel, Manto is widely admired for his analyses of violence, bigotry, prejudice, and the relationships between reason and unreason.

Combining realism with surrealism and irony, Manto's works, such as the celebrated short story Toba Tek Singh, are aesthetic masterpieces that continue to give profound insight into the nature of human loss, violence, and devastation.

Another famous Urdu writer is Ismat Chughtai, whose short story, "Lihaaf" (The Quilt), on a lesbian relationship between an upper-class

Muslim woman and her maidservant created great controversy following its publication in 1942.

Since 1945

Following World War II, the artistic range, and numbers of writers of short stories grew significantly.

Due in part to frequent contributions from John O'Hara, The New Yorker would come to exercise substantial influence as a weekly short story publication for more than half a century.

Shirley Jackson's story, "The Lottery" (1948), elicited the strongest response in the magazine's history to that time. Other frequent contributors during the 1940s included John Steinbeck, Jean Stafford, Eudora Welty, and John Cheever, who is best known for "The Swimmer" (1964), beautifully blending realism and surrealism.

Many other American short story writers greatly influenced the evolving form of the short story. For example, J.D. Salinger's Nine Stories (1953) experimented with point of view and voice, while Flannery O'Connor's well-known story, "A Good Man is Hard to Find" (1955), reinvigorated the Southern Gothic style.

Cultural and social identity played a considerable role in much of the short fiction of the 1960s.[citation needed] Philip Roth and Grace Paley cultivated distinctive Jewish-American voices. Tillie Olsen's "I Stand Here Ironing" (1961) adopted a consciously feminist perspective. James Baldwin's collection, Going to Meet the Man (1965), told stories of African American life.

Science fiction stories with a special poetic touch was a genre developed with great popular success by Ray Bradbury. Stephen King published many sciences fiction short stories in men's magazines in the 1960s and after. King's interest is in the supernatural and macabre.

Donald Barthelme and John Barth produced works in the 1970s that demonstrate the rise of the postmodern short story. While traditionalism maintained a significant influence on the form of the short story, minimalism gained widespread influence in the 1980s, most notably in the work of Raymond Carver and Ann Beattie.

Carver helped usher in an "extreme minimalist aesthetic" and expand the scope of the short story, as did Lydia Davis, through her idiosyncratic and laconic style.

The Argentine writer Jorge Luis Borges is one of the best-known writers of short stories in the Spanish language. "The Library of Babel" (1941) and "The Aleph" (1945) handle difficult subjects like infinity.

Borges won American fame with "The Garden of Forking Paths", published in the August 1948 issue of Ellery Queen's Mystery Magazine.

Two of the most representative writers of the Magical realism genre are also widely known Argentine short story writers, Adolfo Bioy Casares and Julio Cortázar. The Nobel laureate author Gabriel García Márquez and the Uruguayan writer Juan Carlos Onetti are further significant magical realist short story writers from the Hispanic world.

In Brazil, João Antonio made a name for himself by writing about poverty and the favelas. Detective literature there was led by Rubem Fonseca.[citation needed] João Guimarães Rosa wrote short stories in the book Sagarana, using a complex, experimental language based on tales of oral tradition.

The role of the bi-monthly magazine Desh (first published in 1933) was key in development of the Bengali short story. Two of the most popular detective story writers of Bengali literature are Sharadindu Bandyopadhyay (the creator of Byomkesh Bakshi) and Satyajit Ray (the creator of Feluda).

The numbers of 21st-century short story writers run into the thousands. Female short story writers have gained increased critical attention, with British authors exploring modern feminist politics in their writings.

Sales of short-story fiction are strong. In the UK, sales jumped 45% in 2017, driven by collections from international names such as Alice Munro, a high number of new writers to the genre, including famous names like actor Tom Hanks plus those who publish their work using readily accessible, digital tools, and the revival of short story salons such as those held by the short fiction company Pin Drop Studio.

More than 690,000 short stories and anthologies were sold in the UK in 2017, generating £5.88 million, the genre's highest sales since 2010.

Throughout the 2010s, there was frequent speculation about a potential "renaissance"; Sam Baker called it a "perfect literary form for the 21st century".

In 2012, Pin Drop Studio launched what became a regular short story salon, held in London and other major cities. Short story writers who have appeared at the salon to read their work to live audiences include Ben Okri, Lionel Shriver, Elizabeth Day, A.L. Kennedy, William Boyd, Graham Swift, David Nicholls, Will Self, Sebastian Faulks, Julian Barnes, Evie Wylde and Claire Fuller.

Canadian short story writers include Alice Munro, Mavis Gallant and Lynn Coady. In 2013, Alice Munro became the first writer of nothing but short stories to be awarded the Nobel Prize in Literature. Her award-winning short story collections include Dance of the Happy Shades, Lives of Girls, and Women, Who Do You Think You Are? The Progress of Love, The Love of a Good Woman and Runaway.

Chapter 21

Characteristics of a Short Story

As a concentrated, concise form of narrative and descriptive prose fiction, the short story has been theorized about through the traditional elements of dramatic structure: exposition (the introduction of setting, situation, and main characters), complication (the event that introduces the conflict), rising action, crisis (the decisive moment for the protagonist and his commitment to a course of action), climax (the point of highest interest in terms of the conflict and the point with the most action) and resolution (the point when the conflict is resolved).

Because of their length, short stories may or may not follow this pattern. For example, modern short stories only occasionally have an exposition, more typically beginning in the middle of the action (in medias res).

As with longer stories, plots of short stories also have a climax, crisis or turning point.

In general, short stories feature endings which are either conclusive or open-ended.

Ambiguity is a recurrent trope in short stories, whether in their ending, characterization, or length.

As with any art form, the exact characteristics of a short story will vary depending on who is its creator.

Characteristic of short story authors, according to professor of English, Clare Hanson, is that they are "losers and loners, exiles, women, blacks writers who for one reason or another have not been part of the ruling "narrative" or epistemological/experiential framework of their society."

Who wrote the first short story?

Novels, you may be surprised to know, pre-date the first literary short stories by at least a hundred years. The wisdom of the academy would have it that the first true literary short story was Sir Walter Scott's The Two Drovers, issued in 1827 as the second story in The Chronicles of Canongate.

Who defined the short story?

A short story is fictional work of prose that is shorter in length than a novel. Edgar Allan Poe, in his essay "The Philosophy of Composition," said that a short story should be read in one sitting, anywhere from a half hour to two hours.

Who is the famous short story writer?

Ernest Hemingway, American novelist and short-story writer awarded the Nobel Prize for Literature in 1954.

What is the purpose of short story?

Short stories are self-contained works of prose fiction whose function is to impart a moral, capture a moment, or evoke a certain mood. Short stories are often more focused, as all the elements within—plot, character, pacing, story structure, and so on—must work together towards this common goal.

What is the origin of storytelling?

Storytelling originated with visual stories, such as cave drawings, and then shifted to oral traditions, in which stories were passed down from generation to generation by word of mouth. There was then a shift to words formed into narratives, including written, printed, and typed stories.

I hope you enjoyed the refreshing course on this last chapter. I wrote because my students asked for it.

References

"Short story - Emergence of the modern short story | Britannica". www. britannica.com. Retrieved 2023-04-20.

Mitchell 2019, p. 24.

Azhikode, Sukumar (1977). "The Short Story in Malayalam". Indian Literature. 20 (2): 5–22. ISSN 0019-5804. JSTOR 24157289.

Poe, Edgar Allan (1984). Edgar Allan Poe: Essays and Reviews. Library of America. pp. 569–77.

Fatma, Gulnaz A Short History of the Short Story: Western and Asian Traditions Modern History Press 2012, p.2-3

Bunting, Joey (2012). Let's Write a Short Story. thewritepractice.com.

Mitchell 2019, p. 8.

Boyd, William. "A short history of the short story". Retrieved 2018-04-17.

Hayes 2012, p. 71.

Mitchell 2019, p. 3.

Deirdre Fulton (2008-06-11). "Who reads short shorts?". thePhoneix. com. Archived from the original on 2009-08-21. Retrieved 2013-06-06. each of their (less-than-1000-word) stories

Cuddon, J.A. (1999). The Penguin Dictionary of Literary Terms and Literary Theory (3rd ed.). London: Penguin. p. 864. ISBN 9780140513639.

Abrams, M.H. (1999). Glossary of Literary Terms (7th ed.). Orlando, FL: Harcourt Brace. pp. 286–87. ISBN 0-15-505452-X.

"Complete Nebula Awards Rules Including the Ray Bradbury and Andre Norton Awards (Revised & Updated)". sfwa.org. Retrieved 2017-06-27.

Azhikode, Sukumar (1977). "The Short Story in Malayalam". Indian Literature. 20 (2): 5–22. ISSN 0019-5804. JSTOR 24157289.

Short Story in Jacob E. Safra e.a., The New Encyclopædia Britannica, 15th edition, Micropaedia volume 10, Chicago, 1998.

Internet Book List: Book Information: Oxford Book of Gothic Tales.

Winnie Chan The Economy of the Short Story in British Periodicals of the 1890s, Introduction, Routledge 2007

Hayes 2012, p. 70.

"Brander Matthews | American writer | Britannica". www.britannica.com. Retrieved 2022-08-27.

"Britannica Academic". academic.eb.com. Retrieved 2022-12-23.

Hayes 2012, p. 82, 85.

Elizabeth Anne Payne (17 November 2003). Mississippi Women: Their Histories, Their Lives. University of Georgia Press. ISBN 978-0-8203-2502-6. Retrieved 24 July 2012.

Leake, Grace (July 1933). "Blanche Colton Williams, Molder of Literature". Holland's, The Magazine of the South.

Mitchell 2019, p. 6.

Mitchell 2019, p. 6-7.

Mitchell 2019, p. 17, 153.

Young 2018, p. 1.

"Sales of short story collections surge | The Bookseller". www.thebookseller.com. Retrieved 2018-04-17.

Moore, Matthew (27 January 2018). "Short story revival cuts novels down to size". The Times. ISSN 0140-0460.

Young 2018, p. 2.

"Salon society: highbrow nights out – short stories with Pin Drop". Evening Standard. Retrieved 2018-04-17.

Oldfield, Simon (2018-07-12). A Short Affair – anthology of original short fiction, illustrated by Royal Academy artists. ISBN 978-1-4711-4732-6.

Baker, Sam (2014-05-18). "The irresistible rise of the short story. Pin Drop Studio". Daily Telegraph. ISSN 0307-1235. Archived from the original on 2022-01-11. Retrieved 2018-03-21.

"The BBC National Short Story Award 2020 with Cambridge University". BBC Radio 4. Retrieved 24 August 2021.

"V. S. Pritchett Short Story Prize - Royal Society of Literature".

Baker, Sam (2014-05-18). "The irresistible rise of the short story. Pin Drop Studio". Daily Telegraph. ISSN 0307-1235. Archived from the original on 2022-01-11. Retrieved 2018-03-21.

Onwuemezi, Natasha (June 27, 2016). "Fuller wins annual Royal Academy & Pin Drop short story prize". The Bookseller.

"The top short story competitions to enter". The Sunday Times Short Story Awards. 10 February 2017. Archived from the original on 16 August 2017.

"The Nobel Prize in Literature 2013". NobelPrize.org. Retrieved 2019-04-16.

"The Nobel Prize in Literature 2013". NobelPrize.org. Retrieved 2019-04-16.

"Nobel Prize in Literature 1910". Nobel Foundation. Archived from the original on 2008-10-11. Retrieved 2008-10-17.

"Nobel Prize in Literature 1982". Nobel Foundation. Archived from the original on 2008-10-17. Retrieved 2008-10-17.

Young 2018, p. 12.

Young 2018, p. 13.

About the Author

Norma Iris Pagan Morales was born in Ponce, Puerto Rico. She comes from a very lovable family. Her parents, Juan Jose Pagan Rodriguez, and Digna Morales Figueroa, now deceased, always helped her with her projects as a writer and teaching career.

Norma had three siblings, Adelin Milagros Pagan Morales, Juan Jose Pagan Morales, and Julio Manuel Pagan Morales. Julio Manuel Pagan Morales died on September 19, 1998, and my dear sister Adelin Milagros Pagan Morales died on February 17, 2023.

Norma did all her academic studies in New York City, Puerto Rico, and Canada. She worked in the City of New York Police Department. As an Educator, she worked in New York City Bd. Of Education as an English Teacher, in Puerto Rico Bd. of Education as an English teacher and in the Puerto Rico Army National.

She has teaching certifications for English as a Second Language and Teaching English as a Foreign Language.

She had published twenty books: Proud of My Puerto Rican Bequest, ¿Porque Soy Boricua? Poemas del Alma, Art in Written Form, A Baffling Short Stories Collection, On Job in the Big Apple, Puerto Rican Soldiers Serving with Pride, Nature's Rage in the Caribbean, Boricua de Pura Cepa, You are the One, The Unfaithfuls, Christopher Columbus, Violence in the City, Poemas Tiernos, Mis Raices, My Little Sister, Two Stranger and The Wrong Man